the GREAT CANADIAN HOCKEY PHRASE BOOK

PAUL ARSENEAULT

Nimbus Publishing Limited
PO Box 9166
Halifax, NS B3K 5M8
(902) 455-4286

Printed and bound in Canada

Front cover: Heather Bryan
Interior Design: John van der Woude

Library and Archives Canada Cataloguing in Publication

Arseneault, Paul, 1963-

The great Canadian hockey phrase book / Paul Arseneault.

ISBN 13: 978-1-55109-639-1

ISBN 10: 1-55109-639-0

1. Hockey—Terminology. I. Title.

GV847.A88 2007 796.962'014 C2007-905065-4

We acknowledge the financial support of the Government of Canada through the Book Publishing Industry Development Program (BPIDP) and the Canada Council, and of the Province of Nova Scotia through the Department of Tourism, Culture and Heritage for our publishing activities.

Acknowledgements

I would like to thank Nimbus Publishing for the opportunity to write this book and acknowledge Sandra McIntyre and Patrick Murphy, in particular, for their help. I would also like to thank Tom Moore for his research assistance and my family for their support and patience. I would also like to acknowledge Saint Jude, patron saint.

Introduction

How about a little game of word association? What immediately comes to mind when you hear the words "cup," "saucer," and "dish?" If you said that these were all terms from the great game of hockey, then you truly are a bona fide fan of the coolest game on earth. If you said that these were all items you keep in your kitchen, then you need to keep reading and get up to snuff on all the terms and phrases associated with Canada's favourite pastime.

There has always been a special relationship between the English language and sport. In many cases, especially here in North America, terms that originate in local arenas, diamonds, and gridirons find a permanent home in our everyday conversation. Perhaps no sport, though, has a deeper love affair with its lingo than the wonderful sport of hockey.

Over the past one hundred years, the sport that has become known worldwide for its unique combination of finesse and force has also established a reputation for nurturing a jargon that can both enlighten and entertain. In what other sport can an invitation to dance actually mean a rendezvous to rumble? The list of terms and phrases that have added colour and texture to the sport is an impressive one and many have become as much a part of convention as the game itself.

To understand how it was that these sayings became such a permanent and integral part of our culture, we need to first acknowledge that at one point they were all that connected us to our hallowed hockey heroes. From the moment *Hockey Night in Canada* forged its first mass radio audience, over a half-century ago, brilliant broadcasters like Foster Hewitt and Danny Gallivan were using words to create a picture for us so that we, too, might be able to envision the mighty Maurice Richard streaking down the wing or the great Gordie Howe driving to the net.

As the sport of hockey has evolved, so has its language. Every aspect of the game—from strategy to stats, to rules and regulations, to the latest innovations—now has its own directory of definitions that attempts to describe, detail, and depict. In this book I've whittled down a century's worth of commentary and have tried to bring the game alive through the written word. Whether you are an expert or novice to the sport of hockey, you will have surely learned something new about our national sport after you've finished reading *The Great Canadian Hockey Phrase Book.*

A

All-star game

This mid-season classic is designed to showcase the best talent that a league or circuit has to offer. In 2007, the NHL held its fifty-fourth all-star game in Dallas and it was highly anticipated since it would be the first for young superstars Sidney Crosby and Alex Ovechkin. Over the years, the all-star game has been played under various formats, including the very popular "North America versus the World" format from 1998 until 2002.

Alternate captain

You can spot the alternate captain by the "A" that is emblazoned on the upper-left-hand corner of his or her jersey. Normally there are two or three alternate captains per team and their job is to act as the liaison between the on-ice officials and the bench if the captain is unable to do so. In many cases, young players are given an alternate captain position to help them prepare for the day they will be asked to wear the "C."

Alumni

An alumnus is a former member of a particular team. Whether they be amateur or professional, many hockey teams throughout North America have an alumni association made up of former players, coaches, and management.

Artificial ice

Artificial ice is created when cold brine is pumped through pipes just under the surface of the arena floor, freezing the water above the floor. The technique was perfected in the 1870s and brought into general use in the early 1900s.

B

Baby bulls

The "baby bulls" were among a group of eighteen-year-old hockey players who were determined to exercise their legal right to play professional hockey in the late 1970s, in the process proving to be the catalyst for the most important merger in the history of the NHL. Future NHL all-stars Rob Ramage, Rick Vaive, and Michel Goulet were among a group of junior-aged hockey players who went to court in 1978 to establish their right to play with the Birmingham Bulls of the World Hockey Association. The trio won their case and that decision, more than any other, was the impetus for the WHA and the NHL to sign a merger agreement for the 1979–1980 season.

Backhander

Those who saw him play say that Toronto's Dave Keon could shoot a puck on his backhand harder then most could using a snap shot or slapshot. The backhand shot is perhaps the most difficult to master and occurs when a player turns his stick and flips or snaps the puck from the back of the stick blade.

Barn

Hockey teams take pride in defending their home barn, or rink. The word "barn," born out of the fact that many early rinks and arenas across Canada took on the appearance of one, is a term of endearment that belies a sense of pride for many hockey players.

Battle of Alberta

Hockey games that involve the Edmonton Oilers and the Calgary Flames.

Battle of Ontario

Hockey games that involve the Ottawa Senators and the Toronto Maple Leafs.

Battle weary: I think we can excuse the Ottawa Senators for not wanting to meet the Maple Leafs in the Stanley Cup playoffs anytime soon. Since 2000, the Leafs and Senators have hooked up in the post-season four times (2000, 2001, 2002, and 2004) with Toronto winning all four battles.

Beat writer

A beat writer is a journalist assigned to cover a specific sports team. All of the four major sports have beat writers assigned to cover their every move during the season.

Beer league / Rec league

Take heart, hockey players, when all the dreams of playing in the NHL or on our men's or women's national team have begun to fade away, remember there is always the local rec or beer league to show off your talents.

Best of (series)

Most playoff hockey series will either be a best-of-three, best-of-five or best-of-seven game affair. If you are involved in a best-of-seven series (as the NHL uses for playoff matchups) then you need to win four games before your opponent does in order to win the series.

Big Bird

A nickname given to Montreal Canadiens blueliner Larry Robinson. Robinson, along with Serge Savard and Guy Lapointe, formed the "big three" that patrolled the Canadiens blue line and helped them win a number of NHL championships in the 1970s.

Biscuit

A biscuit is another name for the puck. This is a vulcanized piece of rubber, 1-inch thick, 3 inches in diameter, and between 5.5 and 6 ounces in weight. Pucks are frozen before the start of each game to prevent bouncing and can reach speeds of one hundred miles per hour.

Blindsided

A term used to describe a player bodychecked or hit from behind without seeing the opposing player, sometimes resulting in injury. This act usually results in at least a penalty and often a suspension if the hit is thought to be a flagrant foul meant to injure.

Blocked shot

A shot at the goal which is blocked or stopped by anyone or anything other than the goalie. Blocked shots are usually the domain of the defenders, but braver forwards can also get in on the act.

Boarding

When a player checks an opponent from behind violently into the boards it is often called boarding. A boarding infraction can be either a minor penalty or a major penalty depending on the severity of the hit and the type of injury, if any, the victim has sustained.

Bone crusher

There are heavy hitters, and then there are bone crushers. Chris Pronger is a bone crusher and Scott Stevens was the ultimate bone crusher—if you don't believe me, ask Eric Lindros.

Isn't it ironic: If you ask most observers of the NHL who the hardest hitter in the history of the game was, the man who might garner the most votes may very well be Scott Stevens. Stevens would catch unsuspecting players skating through the trolley tracks with their head down and send them on a one-way trip to the moon. Stevens sent more than a few guys to the infirmary concussed, so it is more than a little ironic that Stevens would have to cut short his career because of—you guessed it—post-concussion syndrome.

The Box

If you want to earn yourself more ice time from the coach, then show him or her that you can master both the box and the diamond. Both formations are used to defend the net when your team is short-handed.

The box is used by a team only one player down. In this case, the left forward defends the zone from the left faceoff circle to the blue line and the right forward defends the zone from the right faceoff circle to the blue line. The left defender defends the zone from the left circle to the goal line and the right defender defends the zone from the right faceoff circle to the goal line. The box strategy is designed to keep the puck to the perimeter and to minimize action in the slot or crease.

Box score

Some can't start their day without a steaming cup of coffee. Me, I'm lost until I've read the previous night's NHL box score. The box score is a detailed summary of the previous night's games. Box scores document goals and assists, penalties, shots on goal, starting goaltenders, as well as other pertinent info.

The Brain trust

These men and women are the architects, the builders of the team. The owner, general manager, scouts, front-office personnel, and of course, the coach, all make up the brain trust of a hockey club. It is not a coincidence that franchises like Detroit and New Jersey of the NHL and Halifax and Kelowna of the CHL are perennial winners in their respective leagues. Success always starts at the top by having knowledgeable, experienced, passionate, and capable people guiding the teams year after year.

Buds

Another name for the Toronto Maple Leafs.

? **Trivia:** Believe it or not, the first Toronto-based hockey club to win a Stanley Cup was not the Maple Leafs but rather this team. Can you name it? *Answer on page 121.*

Butt-end / Spear

To butt-end an opponent is to jab them or hit them with the knob end of your stick, while the end of the stick blade is used to spear. Both offences demand an ejection from the game, and are two of the dirtiest plays in hockey.

Butterfly

The butterfly is a popular style goaltenders use to stop the puck. For decades netminders used what is called a standup style, where they relied heavily on their ability to stay upright on their skates and cut down the shooter's scoring angle. Beginning in the 1960s, however, NHL goalies introduced a new style that saw them drop to their knees and spread out in an effort to look big and force shooters to aim high. The butterfly style has now begun a new mutation and more and more young puckstoppers are combining the attributes of the butterfly style with a much more aggressive and acrobatic approach.

Buzzer beater / eye in the sky

New technology means these two hockey terms now go hand in hand. A buzzer beater occurs when a goal is scored just before the buzzer, or siren, sounds to end the period or game. In the old days, it would be a referee's nightmare to have to decide if the puck crossed the line just before or just after the final whistle. Beginning in the early 1990s, however, video replay, or the "eye in the sky" made it certain that the right call would be made each and every time.

? **Eye in the sky:** In the 1992 playoffs, this Detroit Red Wing forward scored the first playoff game-winning goal ever to be determined by video review. Who was that Red Wing? *Answer on page 121.*

C

Calder Trophy

The Calder Memorial Trophy, as it is traditionally called, is awarded annually to the best rookie in the National Hockey League. The trophy is named after Frank Calder, president of the National Hockey League from 1917 to 1943.

Two-sport standout: 1999 Calder Trophy winner Chris Drury was an outstanding baseball player as well as a talented young puckster. In 1989, Drury led his Trumbull, Connecticut, team to a Little League World Series win. Drury would be named tournament MVP and had the honour of meeting the president of the United States.

Cannonading drive

No broadcaster has had a greater impact in terms of influencing the language of the sport than the voice of the Canadiens, Danny Gallivan. One of the terms he coined was "cannonading drive," which was aptly used to describe an extra-hard slapshot.

Gallivanisms: Savardian spinerama, cannonading drive, and scintillating save were all terms that the voice of the Canadiens brought into the game of hockey.

Captain

The captain of a hockey team is usually recognizable by the large "C" he or she is wearing on the upper-left-hand side of the jersey. Contrary to popular opinion, the role of captain is not always given to the most talented or most popular player on the team, but rather the best leader and best communicator. The roles and responsibilities of the captain are as varied as being the liaison between the team and the on-ice officials during the game to being a vocal locker-room presence.

Trivia: Are goalies allowed to be captains? *Answer on page 121.*

Central Scouting Bureau

The NHL's Central Scouting Bureau keeps tabs on the development of junior-aged or entry level hockey players and rates them according to different criteria. NHL clubs rely heavily on Central Scouting for input at draft time. As with many things in sport, rating teenagers is an inexact science and while some players highly rated by Central Scouting have flourished at the pro level, others rated very high have been a bust. For the most part, though, the Central Scouting Bureau is very good at what it does.

Change on the fly

To change lines without waiting for the play to stop. Most line changes are made after a whistle or stoppage of play but to "change on the fly" simply means to change players while the game is taking place. There's always a bit of a risk in doing so, as it is a minor penalty to have too many players on the ice.

Charging

Charging is an infraction called when you take more than two strides before checking an opponent. Charging can be one of the more dangerous actions in a game, as it often leads to checking from behind or high-sticking an opponent.

Cherry picker

Also known as the loafer or the floater, the cherry picker is the player who continually hangs out by the opposition's blue line waiting for the one perfect stretch pass that is going to spring him or her on a breakaway.

Chin music

Bobby Hull, the man of the one hundred mile an hour slapshot, would admit to playing a little chin music early in hockey games. Chin music is a term used to describe a shot up near the head of the goalie in an attempt to intimidate. Hull would often make his first shot a screamer at the head of the opposing goalie in an effort to "send a message."

Century club: Shooting a puck one hundred miles an hour may not be news in the era of composite sticks and power-shooting schools, but in the 1960s being able to shoot a puck over one hundred clicks was a phenomenon. Bobby Hull absolutely wowed a generation of hockey fans when he was able to hit and then surpass the mark during his stint in Chicago.

Choke

This is a term that hockey teams try to avoid like the plague. To choke is to be devoid of killer instinct. If your team has a propensity to let teams back into a game or series when they should have been easily beaten, then the team might soon be tagged with the dreaded "choke" label.

Cinderella team

It seems that in every post-season there is one team that comes out of nowhere to surprise everyone with their winning ways. The Cinderella team is the squad that doesn't impress much during the regular season but catches fire during the playoffs and defeats superior teams on its way to a berth in the final. Unfortunately, for some teams, the clock eventually strikes twelve and the Cinderella story is brought back to reality. For precious few others, like the teams mentioned below, the story ends with a championship banner and a place in hockey lore.

Cinderella story: Unlike the NBA and NFL and even major league baseball, the National Hockey League has been fertile territory for the Cinderella story. In 1993, the Montreal Canadiens had a very unspectacular season by their standards, finishing with 102 points, only fourth best in the conference. After losing their first two post-season games to Quebec, the Canadiens caught fire. Montreal would lose only two more games the entire post-season, and won ten consecutive overtime games, a record which probably will never be broken.

Clear the track

"Clear the track, here comes Shack" was a popular saying in the 1960s and 1970s. Eddie Shack was the consummate showman and not a bad scrapper either in his heyday. Shack went on to greater fame as the spokesperson for "The Pop Shoppe" after his playing days were over.

Closed-door session / players-only meeting

Teams will often turn to a closed-door session when things are not going particularly well and it is time to air differences and frustrations. Closed-door sessions are generally frowned upon, but there are times when players will take the initiative and organize a session where the players and only the players will discuss matters.

Clutch and grab

A term used to describe a close-checking style of game. The clutch and grab became a staple of less-skilled teams in the late 1990s to slow down more talented sides.

Coach's corner

Perhaps no five-minute segment in television garners as much attention as the CBC's "Coach's Corner" segment on *Hockey Night in Canada*. Hosted by Ron MacLean and Don Cherry, the program deals with a variety of hockey-related issues and can be as controversial as it is entertaining. As a testament to Cherry's popularity in Canada, the Kingston, Ontario, native was among the top ten in "The Greatest Canadian" contest.

Colour barrier

Hockey had its own colour barrier to contend with in the early to middle part of the last century until a Maritimer broke through. Willie O'Ree, a fast-skating forward from Fredericton, was called up to the parent Boston Bruins on January 18, 1958, to become the first black athlete to play in the NHL.

Commissioner

The commissioner is the top administrator in the National Hockey League. Everything from rule changes to contract negotiations with the NHLPA eventually ends up in the commissioner's jurisdiction. Although the commissioner is employed by the owners, they will almost always defer to his expertise on such matters. The NHL has only ever had one commissioner (Gary Bettman). Before Bettman's hiring in the fall of 1992, the boss had always been called the president.

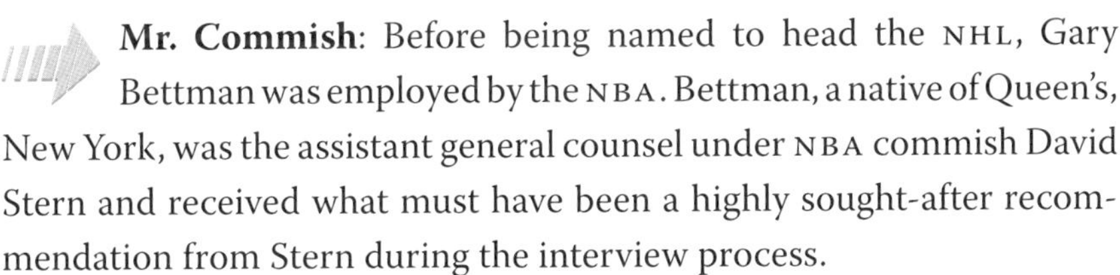

Mr. Commish: Before being named to head the NHL, Gary Bettman was employed by the NBA. Bettman, a native of Queen's, New York, was the assistant general counsel under NBA commish David Stern and received what must have been a highly sought-after recommendation from Stern during the interview process.

Cooperalls

A blast from the past. The 1980s were a decade of change and evolution in the game of hockey and although it was a short-lived phenomenon, Cooperalls were seen as a big step forward at the time. Cooperalls were, of course, the one-piece hockey pants that, for a time, threatened to replace the hockey pants we are now accustomed to seeing. Cooperalls went from hip to ankle and consisted of a girdle and protective pads.

? **Trivia**: Only two NHL teams abandoned the old-style short pants for the longer one-piece Cooperalls. Who were they? *Answer on page 121.*

Corporate sponsor

When a large company gets involved in the financing of a team or a league, they are a corporate sponsor. Over the past few decades, the role of corporate sponsors in the NHL has grown immensely. Through their acquisition of suites, purchase of season tickets, and advertising, corporate sponsors have become a major source of income for the league.

Counterattack

If you turn over the puck in the neutral zone or in your own zone often enough, opponents will eventually burn you with their counterattack. A counterattack is the opposition's ability to mount an offensive thrust once they've regained possession of the puck.

CPR line

The media blitz surrounding Rimouski's Sidney Crosby and his linemates, Marc-Antoine Pouliot and Dany Roussin, in 2004–05 was unparalleled in the history of junior hockey and it has made the trio the most famous CHL line of all-time.

Television, radio, and print media across North America and Europe documented these young men's scoring exploits and they became hockey's main attraction as the NHL struggled through a lockout. Pouliot, Roussin, and Crosby dominated QMJHL opponents as they led their Océanic to a berth in the final of the Memorial Cup, with Crosby taking home the CHL Player of the Year Award for the second consecutive season.

Where are they now?: Sidney Crosby, as you probably know, became a Pittsburgh Penguin in 2005 and has scored at least one hundred points in each of his first two seasons in the NHL becoming the youngest player in the history of the league to score two hundred career points. Marc-Antoine Pouliot is an Edmonton Oiler and after having a strong second half of the season in 2007, looks to have established himself as a solid NHL citizen. Roussin split the 2006–2007 season between Manchester of the AHL and Reading of the ECHL.

Crease

The area directly in front of the goalie where opposing players are not supposed to venture. On most ice surfaces, the crease is easily recognized by the blue paint used to designate it as an off-limits zone. Of course if a penalty was called every time an opponent put a toe in the crease, clubs would never have the opportunity to play five on five, so referees use their common sense when it comes to determining if a player is impeding the goalie. Basically, if a player is in the crease but does not interfere with the goalie's ability to play the puck then no minor infraction is called, but if the player does sufficiently interfere with the goalie's ability to play the puck, then a two minute "goalie interference" call is made.

Cross-crease feed

To pass the puck from one corner of the crease straight through to the other side where a teammate will be waiting for the two-foot tap in.

Crossover

A skating technique that helps skaters measure their balance and mobility. To begin the crossover drill, simply find a spot on the ice and stand still with your skates shoulder-width apart. Now lift your right skate and cross it over your left and bring your left skate underneath your right and back to its original position. Begin this drill by being slow and deliberate—once you become comfortable with the action, you can pick up speed. The crossover can be done left to right or right to left and even back to front and front to back when you have become really adept.

Crowding the crease

This term is used to describe a gaggle of players congregating in front of the net to obscure the goalie's view of the puck.

The Cut

Perhaps no day is as nerve-racking to a hockey player as the day that the final rosters are posted. For those who "make the cut," it means they've survived the tryouts and have earned a place on the club. For those who have failed to make the cut at some point in their hockey careers, don't lose heart, as some of hockey's biggest stars have felt the sting of having failed to make the cut.

Cutting down the angle

Today's goalies work at shutting down the lower part of the net by employing a butterfly style but traditionally, guarding a net was all about cutting down a shooter's angle. To cut down the angle, a goalie moves out of the net and toward the shooter in order to reduce the amount of net the shooter has to aim at.

Cycle

The strategy of cycling the puck became more popular as forwards got more physically imposing and could use their sheer size to keep the puck away from defenders as they methodically worked the puck deep in the offensive zone. Centres and wingers take turns protecting the puck as they inch toward the scoring area between the faceoff circles. With the enactment of the new rules that explicitly deny defenders the ability to impede a forward's progress by holding the body or stick, it is virtually impossible for the defending team to separate forechecking forwards from the puck if an effective cycle is in progress.

D

Dance

When two players decide to square off and drop their gloves, then we have a dance, or fight, on our hands. Normally, officials will not intervene until the combatants are tired or until one fighter is getting a substantial advantage over the other. Once a fight is over, the referee will administer a five-minute major penalty to each player and an additional two minutes to any player he deems to have been an instigator.

McSorley versus Probert: Anyone who saw this dance realized the second it was finished that it was possibly the greatest fight in the history of the NHL. Pittsburgh's Marty McSorley and Detroit's Bobby Probert had been considered two of the top fighters of their day, but it was hard to ever remember an eventful scrap involving them fighting each other. That all changed on February 4, 1994. In a game between the Penguins and Red Wings in Detroit, McSorley and Probert threw haymakers at each other for what seemed like eternity.

In the end, Probert won the decision but McSorley gained a boatload of respect for standing toe to toe with the Wings number 24. Unbelievably, the fight would last nearly two minutes and when it was over both Probert and McSorley, absolutely gassed from the tussle, gave each other a tap on the head as a sign of respect and slowly made their way to the penalty box having solidified their rightful place among the legends of NHL tough guys.

Dangle

Sidney Crosby can dangle, Alexei Kovalev can dangle, and now Alex Ovechkin, he can really dangle. Have you ever noticed how some hockey players seem to have the puck glued to their stick or how they seem to have the ability to stickhandle in a phone booth? Well, it is because they have the God-given talent to dangle. It is almost mesmerizing to watch a player like Ovechkin show the defender the puck and then take it away at the last moment as he blows by. Here is a tip to increase your ability to dangle: practise stickhandling with a tennis ball—it will increase your hand-eye coordination, and that is the real key to being a top-notch dangler.

Dead puck era

The "dead ball era" in baseball describes a time when the pitchers ruled and offence was at a premium. From 1900 to 1920, America's favourite pastime was prone to low-scoring affairs with little in the way of offensive fireworks. The great game of hockey also went through a span where defence was king and high-scoring games were an aberration, and we don't have to go back nearly as far in history to locate it. Hockey's "dead puck era" lasted from the early 1990s right through to the 2003–2004 season. Teams during this period seemed to have a very simple blueprint for success: score early, then stifle the opposition and hang on for a 1–0 or 2–1 victory.

Teams throughout the NHL implemented, then perfected, a defensive "trapping" strategy during this time and the run-and-gun games of the 1980s where 8–7 shootouts were the order of the day instead became a distant memory. It wasn't until some much-needed rule changes, brought in at the beginning of the 2005–2006 campaign, were installed that fans finally saw an uptick in scoring. The "trap," if not eliminated, had at least become less effective.

Deferred salary

The days when professional hockey players signed contracts for five hundred dollars and a team jacket are long gone. Today's contracts can be very complicated and the option of deferring salary is just one example. Because teams have a salary cap that they must now abide by, deferred salaries are becoming very popular. Under a contract with deferred salary, a player agrees to receive a portion of their salary at a point after they have actually earned it.

Defunct franchise

A defunct franchise is one that has folded or has been relocated to another city. Often the owner of a franchise that is struggling will sell the team with the understanding that the team will eventually move to another locale. At times, as in the case of Denver and Minneapolis, the city will be successful in attracting a new franchise at a later date.

Deke

Please allow me to wax poetic:

To fake out a defender with the puck is to deke
A disappearing act with the puck, so to speak
You make him go one way and the puck goes another
Leave him down on all fours mumbling, "what happened, brother?"

Delayed offside

A delayed offside occurs when the puck is shot in over the blue line, trapping a teammate in the offensive zone. The referee will blow the play dead if the offensive team touches the puck or if the offensive team cannot leave the zone in a timely fashion.

The Diamond

As complicated as the box may seem, the diamond is as simple as it gets in terms of hockey strategy. Trying to stop the opposing team from scoring when your team is short-handed by two players is tough, but a little strategy called the diamond actually works quite well. In a nutshell, the two defenders patrol the area from the low slot to the faceoff dots and try to keep everything to the perimeter while the third penalty killer is planted in the high slot taking away that prime scoring area and forcing shots from the blue line.

Whether you are using the "box" or the "diamond," confidence that your goalie is going to stop long shots is a must. As they say, ultimately your best penalty killer must be your keeper!

Digger

A "digger" is a term used to describe a hard-working player who is especially tenacious on the forecheck. While the finesse player will always receive more accolades for his or her scoring or playmaking prowess, the digger is an essential ingredient to any winning hockey club.

Directing the puck

The ability to play the puck with your skate is a most valuable skill. Hockey players who become adept at being able to kick the puck up to their stick or (deftly) accept a hard pass with a skate blade are truly special. Because of their love of soccer, European hockey players seem to be ahead of North American hockey players when it comes to both footwork and the ability to play the puck with their skates.

There is a limit as to what you can do legally with your skates. It is an offence to knowingly kick the puck with your skate into the net. There is a common misconception that the puck cannot hit a skate before going in the net for a goal—this is not true. As long as a player is not purposely using his or her skate to direct the puck into the net, the goal will stand.

Dive

In hockey, perhaps the most unflattering thing a person can be called is a diver. A dive occurs when a player flops to the ice in an attempt to sucker the referee into giving an opposing player a penalty. More often than not, if a player is getting frustrated with the tight checking of an opponent, he or she may try to get his or her nemesis off the ice by pretending to have been tripped, hooked, or interfered with. This can be a two-edged sword, however, as officials have the right to call a penalty (for unsportsmanlike conduct) on a player they feel has been guilty of diving.

It'll cost ya: The NHL was so fed up that in 2003 they began administering fines to chronic divers (those who dove more than once in a season) and posted their names on dressing rooms throughout the NHL as a way to curtail embellishment.

Doghouse

If you are in your coach's doghouse then you either have your fanny firmly stapled to the bench during the game or you find yourself a healthy scratch more often than not. When a coach is not happy with your play or attitude, he may try to send you a message by drastically cutting your playing time or by making you feel less and less like you are part of the equation.

Coaching legend Scotty Bowman was famous for sending players to the doghouse for extended periods of time and then recalling them from exile at a critical moment in the season and giving them an opportunity to redeem themselves. Bowman's philosophy, which was usually right on the money, was that the player would be so angry at Bowman and so anxious to prove Bowman wrong, that the player would go through a wall to prove his worth and would usually go on to play his best hockey of the season.

Donnybrook

'Twas a time when the donnybrook was as common in a hockey game as a highlight-reel goal or spectacular save. In the era of the Broad Street Bullies of Philadelphia, or the big bad Bruins of Boston, the donnybrook, or hockey brawl, as it is also known, was a common occurrence. The evolution of the game over the past two decades, however, has made the donnybrook nothing more than a thing of hockey lore. Although some might miss the sight of gloves and sticks strewn about the ice surface while Dave "The Hammer" Schultz and Dave "Tiger" Williams went toe to toe for what seemed like hours, I think we can all agree it is a part of the game better left behind.

The brawl in Montreal: If you're looking for one particular moment where the NHL realized it had to do something about its image as a violent sport, you'll find it among the chaos of a second period brawl between bitter provincial rivals the Quebec Nordiques and the Montreal Canadiens on April 20, 1984. While the playoff series should have been known for the play of stars like Quebec's Peter Stastny and Montreal's Mats Naslund, it will forever be remembered for a career-ending punch to the face of an unsuspecting Canadiens rearguard.

For days, the image of Montreal Canadiens defenceman Jean Hamel crumpled on the ice and knocked cold by a punch from Quebec forward Louis Sleigher was the focus of television sports shows throughout North America. The bench-clearing brawl was a black eye on a sport that was already receiving much negative press south of the border. To his credit, NHL president John Ziegler seized the opportunity to bring about change, promising to finally shed the league of its propensity for allowing skill and finesse to be overshadowed by the actions of so-called enforcers.

Dots

The dots sprinkled on the playing surface are used primarily for faceoffs. There are two dots in each defending zone and five additional dots in the neutral zone, including the one at centre ice. Hash marks, the perpendicular lines used as a guide to position players, accompany each dot.

Down low

"Working the puck down low" is a strategy that became popular with the use of mammoth forwards, who could use their sheer size to keep the puck away from defenders as they methodically worked the puck along the boards. Centres and wingers take turns protecting the puck as they inch toward the scoring area between the dots.

With the enactment of the new rules that explicitly deny defenders the ability to impede a forward's progress by holding the body or stick, it is virtually impossible for the defending team to separate forechecking forwards from the puck if an effective cycle is in progress.

Draft choice

Each June, the National Hockey League holds its entry draft. The draft is important, as it allows teams to replenish talent or replace players who have moved to different teams or who have retired from the game. Players are selected on a round-by-round basis and can either sign a contract with the club that selects them or remain unsigned and become eligible for future drafts. By far the vast majority of drafted players come from the CHL, North America's major junior league, although American college players have been getting selected more often in the past decade or so.

Hit and miss: To say that drafting teenagers is an inexact science is an understatement. More often than not number one selections like Mario Lemieux and Sidney Crosby come as advertised and make their clubs instantly better, but first-round picks like Minnesota's Brian Lawton in 1983 and Atlanta's Patrick Stefan in 1999 prove that they don't always work out as planned.

Drag the skate

There are two uses for this phrase. To "drag the skate" is to stay onside by dragging a skate along the blue line, but it also describes digging the skate into the ice so as to assist stopping.

Drill

Take in any minor hockey practice and you'll see a coach putting his charges through a series of drills designed to improve skating, shooting, and passing ability. Drills are purposely repetitive in an attempt to make the skills almost second nature to the athlete. A recent change in the North American approach to practices has replaced repetitive drills with an emphasis on creative play.

Meeting of the minds: In 1999, in the wake of a number of disappointing finishes in international play, Hockey Canada held a summit on the state of hockey in Canada. One of the more popular suggestions at the meeting was to stop emphasizing specific systems to youngsters and allow them to get back to expressing themselves creatively on the ice. The results were immediate at almost every level of Canadian hockey, most notably a three-peat by Canada's national junior team (2005–2007).

Drop pass

Analysts will tell you that this is the riskiest play in hockey. The drop pass is accomplished when the puck carrier passes the puck backwards to a teammate. Although I am not aware of any stats measuring the success rate of the drop pass, a botched drop pass will most certainly mean a great scoring chance for the other team.

Dynasty

Generally thought to be a team or franchise that wins four or more consecutive Stanley Cup championships. The New York Islanders were the latest dynasty, having won four Cups in a row from 1980 to 1983. The Montreal Canadiens have created dynasties in two different eras, having won four straight championships from 1976 through 1979 and an amazing five consecutive titles from 1956 to 1960.

Dynasty denied: No team has ever equalled the Canadiens' record of five titles in a row, although the Edmonton Oilers of the 1980s would have, had it not been for a bizarre and heartbreaking goal. The Oilers, behind Gretzky, Messier, and Fuhr, had won the Stanley Cup in 1984 and 1985 and were primed to win it all again in 1986 but were derailed by a stunning turn of events in game seven of the Smythe Division finals against Calgary. Rookie defenceman Steve Smith, celebrating his twenty-third birthday, banked a clearing pass off Edmonton keeper Grant Fuhr and into his own net. The Flames would go on to win the game and deny the Oilers the expected three-peat. The Oilers would recover to win cups in 1987 and 1988.

E

Eating the puck

Sometimes a player needs to take a hit in order to make a play. One such case is when a defender is forced to eat the puck. If a defender has possession of the puck along the boards, and a forechecker bearing down, then the defender may be forced to absorb the hit and protect the puck at all costs.

Empty-net goal

A goal scored into an empty net when the keeper has been removed in exchange for an extra attacker.

End to end

Going end to end describes a sparkling offensive play where an athlete carries the puck uninterrupted from his own end all the way to the opposing team's end, sometimes resulting in a goal. A spectacular end-to-end rush, especially when a goal is scored, is one of those plays in hockey that brings fans out of their seats.

Equalizer

The equalizer in hockey is the goal that ties the game.

Expansion

The European invasion, multi-million-dollar contracts, eighty-two-game seasons—all these innovations and more can eventually be traced back to the most important expansion in the history of professional hockey. In 1967, the NHL joined the NFL, NBA, and MLB as elite North American sports leagues with an expansion that saw the league set up shop in six American cities from the Atlantic to the Pacific. Philadelphia, Pittsburgh, St Louis, Minnesota, Oakland, and Los Angeles would expand the league to twelve teams and bring new-found enthusiasm and optimism to the league. New, charismatic owners like Los Angeles's Jack Kent Cooke forced the NHL to view its sport in a different way, and the new entries helped the NHL carve out a niche in the North American sports scene that it enjoys to this day.

Mega-merger: In 1979, the NHL experienced its last great expansion with four teams coming into the league from the WHA. The Hartford Whalers, Quebec Nordiques, Winnipeg Jets, and Edmonton Oilers were solid hockey entities that were welcomed with open arms to the NHL fraternity. Of course, the biggest name to come over from the WHA was "The Great One," Wayne Gretzky. After beginning his pro hockey career in Indianapolis, Gretzky would eventually move on to Alberta and become the greatest hockey player in the history of the game. Unfortunately, of the WHA teams to join the NHL, only Gretzky's Oilers would survive the financial realities of the sport in the 1990s as Quebec, Winnipeg, and Hartford relocated to Colorado, Phoenix, and North Carolina, respectively.

F

Face mask

All the goalies out there need to take a moment to thank Jacques Plante for the fact that they have all of their teeth and no facial scars. The face mask is the protective mask a goaltender wears to prevent injury from errant pucks, sticks, skates, and other projectiles. The vast majority of goalies today wear either a carbon fibre mask or a fibreglass-Kevlar mask. A few goalies, though, including Dominik Hasek and Chris Osgood, still prefer to wear the birdcage-style mask first introduced to North America in the late 1970s. Of course, netminders did not always wear a mask, that was until the day Plante took an Andy Bathgate shot to the head and decided to defy Montreal management and don the disguise.

Fashion statement: Today, having a cool paint job on your mask seems almost as important as the mask's ability to withstand a hundred mile-an-hour slapshot. Beginning in the mid-1970s, goalies began to use their masks as an avenue for creative expression. Although a few masks worn by contemporary keepers are noteworthy in terms of their artistic impression, it was a couple of masks from the 1970s that are the most memorable. Anyone who has ever seen Gilles Gratton's lion mask from the 1977 season or Gerry Cheever's "stitches" mask from that same era will tell you that it was some of the best and most unique mask artwork.

Faceoff

Play begins or resumes in hockey with a faceoff. The referee makes sure that players on both teams are in their proper positions and, once satisfied, drops the puck between opposing centres.

Face wash

Not only does a face wash go against all sporting etiquette, it can also land you in the penalty box for a couple of minutes. The face wash is accomplished by rubbing your glove in the face of an opponent.

Falling on the puck

This is one of the areas of the game where on-ice officials need to apply sound judgement. Intentionally falling on the puck so as to impede the ability of an opponent to get possession is a minor offence. If a player gathers a puck under his body while lying in the crease, then the referee will instead award a penalty shot.

Fantasy league

Not every hockey fan can be an NHL general manager, but fantasy hockey leagues allow every one of us to try our hand at creating, developing, and administering a hockey club. "Fantasy Leagues"—quickly becoming a huge business in North America—allow you to draft, trade, and sign players for a price and is usually administered online or through a local media outlet.

Farm team

A farm team is one of a plethora of minor league professional teams that supply players to the National Hockey League. Clubs that have an affiliation with NHL teams are considered to be farm teams.

Blueprint for success: Without debate, the most successful minor pro league is the American Hockey League (AHL). The AHL, which has teams in both the U.S. and Canada, has been around in some form for almost a century. Current league president David Andrews has done an outstanding job since he took over the helm in the mid-1990s and few circuits have been able to equal the AHL's success over that time.

Fast ice

Fast ice describes very hard and glassy ice which is smooth with no cracks, lumps, or mushy spots. When ice is smooth and hard like this, skates glide over it more easily, allowing a skater to skate more freely.

Worst and best: In a recent poll, Rexall Place, home to the Edmonton Oilers, was thought to have the best ice in the NHL while Madison Square Garden, the home of the Rangers, was thought to have the worst.

Feather pass

Also known as the saucer pass, the feather pass was a trademark of the greatest player of them all. Wayne Gretzky was unbelievable at being able to lift the puck over the blade of an opponent's stick and have it land perfectly on the tape of a teammate's twig. The key component to making the feather pass work is timing, as the pass only works if it can land on the tape of a teammate already in motion.

Dynamic duo: Arguably the best twosome to ever suit up together, Wayne Gretzky and Finland's Jari Kurri were special during their time together on the Oilers and Kings. The image of Gretzky feeding Kurri an immaculate feather pass in the slot and Kurri accepting it and wiring it to the top shelf is still etched in the minds of many hockey fans.

Five for fighting

This is the amount of penalty time players receive for a fighting major.

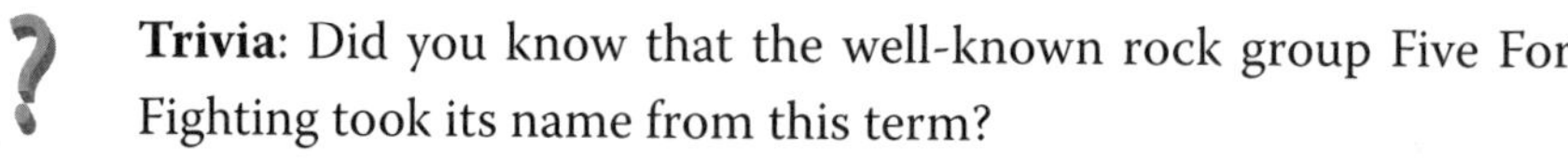

Trivia: Did you know that the well-known rock group Five For Fighting took its name from this term?

Five hole

The area between the goalie's pads that is left open as he or she crouches into the butterfly position to make a save. If you shoot and score between a goalie's legs before he can close his pads then you have scored in the "five hole." The number one and two "holes" are the top left and right of the net, respectively, and the three and four positions are the bottom left and right, respectively.

Five-player unit

This is a strategy for breaking out of your defensive zone. For example, if your defenceman has the puck behind your net and wants to break-out as a five-player unit, then the wingers need to have their backsides up against the boards perpendicular to the faceoff dots, the centre comes back and circles wide to either side and the other defenceman needs to support his or her partner by finding an open spot near the puck carrier.

By breaking out in this way, the defender has a number of options in order to clear the zone and begin the attack. The advantages of breaking out as a five-player unit include the fact that there is plenty of support on the rush and immediate help in case there is a turnover. The main disadvantage of breaking out this way is that it does not stretch the defending team and allows the opposition plenty of time to get back and defend. A five-player breakout also creates a lot of traffic in the neutral zone and that can lead to costly turnovers.

Flamingo

Players act like a flamingo when they race out to black a shot only to raise one leg like a flamingo at the last second so as to avoid taking the shot on the shin or ankle. Every goaltender would rather their team-mates not even make the attempt to block the shot if they are only going to "flamingo" at the last moment because the goalie ends up getting screened, or blocked out, in the process.

Flopper

A "flopper" is used to describe a goalie who dives or flops to the ice to make a save. Usually floppers do not have a long shelf life because shooters will start aiming high. Perhaps the most famous flopper was the “Gumper,” Lorne Worsley, who had a Hall of Fame career with Montreal and Minnesota, among other teams.

Worsley’s wisdom: Yogi Berra wasn’t the only sports legend to come up with some noteworthy quotes. Gump Worsley had some gems of his own. When he was playing with the Rangers, Gump was asked what team gave him the most trouble. His reply was, “the New York Rangers.”

Forward lines

Hockey teams consist of three or four forward lines and these lines are made up of a centre along with a left wing and a right wing. Normally the first line is the most talented line and it tends to see more ice time than the other three. The second line is often a skilled line as well, often on par with the first line in terms of ability and talent. The third line is often a checking line or defensive line dispatched to play against the other team’s top line. The fourth line is usually an energy line that does not see much ice time, but is used periodically to introduce some energy and excitement by the coach if the team appears lethargic.

Franchise player

Sidney Crosby, Alex Ovechkin, and Roberto Luongo are all examples of franchise players. A franchise player is the athlete that best represents the identity of a team and is its undisputed leader. The franchise player is the face of a team and in some cases, as with Crosby and Ovechkin, can be the face of an entire league.

What’s in a name: The franchise player’s impact on a team is not only measured in wins and losses. The market value of a team can rise dramatically with the arrival of a franchise player to the team roster. The value of franchises like Pittsburgh, Washington, and Vancouver depends a great deal on the presence of Crosby, Ovechkin, and Luongo, respectively.

The French Connection

The Beatles had their George Harrison, the Three Tenors had their José Carreras, and the French Connection had René Robert. While Gilbert Perreault and Richard Martin became the darlings of the Buffalo sports media in the 1970s, Robert quietly went about his job as the heart and soul of one of the more prolific lines ever to play in the National Hockey League.

Compared to the gaudy numbers that both Perreault and Martin were able to post, it is understandable how Robert's two forty-goal seasons and his single one hundred-point season might get lost in the shuffle, but make no mistake about it, Robert was the epitome of skill and grit and created a lot of room for his mates during their time together on the Sabres. Perhaps the most upsetting thing is that despite their outstanding careers, they never had the opportunity to hoist Lord Stanley's Cup above their heads.

Front office

The front office is sometimes called the brain trust. The front office includes the general manager, assistant general manager, scouts, and player personnel offices. The front office is often in charge of the day-to-day operations and, in the case of professional hockey teams, the front office is sometimes broken up into separate hockey and business operations.

Frozen Four

The Frozen Four is college hockey's answer to the Final Four. The Frozen Four hockey tournament is the semifinals and finals for both men's and women's NCAA hockey. The tournament began in 1948 with Michigan beating Dartmouth and has produced a winner every year since. The 2007 men's winner was Michigan State while the University of Wisconsin (Madison) won the women's title.

Full strength

If a team is playing at full strength, they are playing with five skaters (two wingers, a centre, two defencemen, and a goalkeeper). Goalies can be removed from the net at any time and replaced with another skater.

G

Game-winning goal

The rule governing game-winning goals is not as straightforward as you might think, but in essence if your team wins 4–2 and you scored your team's third goal, then you will be credited with the game-winning goal.

Garbage collector

If you're a forward who likes to plant yourself in the middle of the opponent's crease just waiting to pounce on a juicy rebound, then you are a garbage collector. If you don't mind getting mauled by opposing defencemen while you stand on the doorstep anticipating banging home a free puck, then you're a garbage collector. And if all of your goals are scored from within six feet of the net, then yes, you are indeed a garbage collector.

One man's trash is another man's treasure: The garbage collector often toils in the shadow of the superstar while paying a hefty physical price for his or her efforts, but just in case you thought it was not worth the sacrifice, remember that Steve Shutt (Canadiens), Phil Esposito (Blackhawks, Bruins, and Rangers), and Bobby Clarke (Flyers) all made it to the Hockey Hall of Fame doing exactly that.

Gathering of the clans

A phrase to describe players pushing and shoving and getting involved in a scrum.

Getting tossed

Getting tossed means to be kicked out of the game. There are numerous ways to find yourself being shown the exit—everything from a game misconduct penalty for fighting or attempting to injure another player to vehemently arguing an official's call.

Give-and-go

This term is used to describe a type of breakout play that demands a keen sense of timing and passing precision. The give-and-go happens when a player passes the puck to a teammate who is relatively stationary. The passer then skates up the ice and past the opposing checker as he prepares to receive a return pass.

Glass

Not the glass you might be accustomed to at home, hockey arenas use Plexiglas placed atop the boards that can take the force of pucks and bodies slamming up against it without breaking. Seamless glass has been introduced to eliminate the need for metal borders, a common fixture in older arenas.

Goals-against average

The goals-against average (GAA) measures the average number of goals allowed per game by the goaltender.

Goaltender factory

The "Q" has long been regarded as a treasure trove of outstanding young goaltending talent. Conn Smythe Award–winning goalkeepers Patrick Roy and J. S. Giguere cut their teeth in the QMJHL, while Olympic hero and perennial Vezina Trophy candidate Martin Brodeur also starred in the league.

Gobble the puck

Usually reserved for goalkeepers, this term means to retrieve or cover up a loose puck.

Golden Jet

Better known as Bobby Hull, the Golden Jet is considered by many to be the best left winger to ever play in the National Hockey League. In just over 1,000 NHL games, Hull scored 610 goals and 560 assists for an impressive 1,170 total points.

A million reasons: Few seriously thought Bobby Hull would ever jump ship and leave Chicago of the NHL for the fledgling World Hockey Association. In the fall of 1972, having been offered a salary he could not refuse (a million dollars over ten years), Hull began play with the new league's Winnipeg Jets and number 9 gave the WHA instant credibility. Hull would finish his pro hockey career in 1979–1980 as a member of the NHL's Hartford Whalers.

The Gondola

The gondola is the nickname given to the broadcast booth that housed the most famous announcer in NHL history, Foster Hewitt.

Ballard's blooper: Harold Ballard, the late owner of the Maple Leafs, did many things to rile fans of Toronto's NHL club, but when he tore down Hewitt's beloved gondola in 1979 to make way for private boxes, it was the last straw in the eyes of many of the Leafs' faithful.

Goon

I am going to take this moment to correct a common mistake that hockey fans and observers alike tend to make: a goon and an enforcer are not the same thing. Unlike the enforcer, the goon has zero hockey talent to go along with an unquenchable thirst for fighting. Enforcers, you see, can be great fighters and still find themselves useful fourth line and special teams players who will pot the occasional goal for their clubs. The goon, on the other hand, cannot skate, cannot pass, and makes no pretense to having any other desire than to hurt any player wearing a different coloured jersey.

Allow me to illustrate: Bobby Probert was arguably the best enforcer there ever was. Zdeno Chara, perhaps the toughest hombre in the NHL today, is an all-star enforcer who also wears the "C" in Boston. On the other hand, ex-Maple Leaf Jim Korn and the late Steve "The Missing Link" Durbano were one hundred percent solid-gold goons.

Goose egg / doughnut

A "goose egg" or "doughnut" is a term used to describe a shutout.

Gordie Howe hat trick

While a hat trick in hockey is most commonly considered scoring three goals in one game, it is the Gordie Howe hat trick that best exemplifies being a scorer, a playmaker, and a tough guy. If you've just scored a Gordie Howe hat trick, then you have scored a goal, had an assist, and taken part in a fight in the same game. Mr. Hockey, as Howe was known, could do it all and that included mixing it up with the opposition when the situation called for it. Gordie Howe played professional hockey for parts of six decades and was a six-time NHL MVP.

Go-to player

As it is with most sports, the go-to player in hockey is that one special player teams turn to when they need a big goal or save.

H

Habs

The Montreal Canadiens are well known by this nickname in English-speaking Canada. The word is derived from the term "Les Habitants" and refers to farmers that worked the land along the St. Lawrence River from 1700 to the beginning of the twentieth century.

Hacker

A hacker is a player who is careless, if not dangerous, with his or her stick. A hacker will slash, cross check, spear, and use the stick in any number of ways to create space and make the opposition think twice about getting too close. Edmonton superstar Glenn Anderson was a notorious hacker who was worth a goal or a gash on almost every shift.

Hang up the blades

Another way of saying that someone is retiring from the game.

Hardware

Another name for trophies or awards.

Hart Trophy

The trophy presented annually to the most valuable player in the NHL. The trophy is voted on by the Professional Hockey Writers' Association and is not to be confused with the Lester B. Pearson Trophy, which is selected by the players' association. Players who have won the award more than once include Mark Messier, Dominik Hasek, and Guy Lafleur.

All Hart: Sidney Crosby won his first Hart Trophy in 2007 and it may not even have been his biggest honour in that year. Exactly two weeks before his MVP win, the Nova Scotia native was named the new captain of the Pittsburgh Penguins.

Hash marks

The hash marks are two pairs of parallel lines on either side of the faceoff circles in both ends of the rink.

Hatchetman

Another name for a hacker.

Head coach / assistant coach

It wasn't all that long ago that most teams had only one coach behind the bench and he or she had little need, nor much use, for the plethora of assistants that seem to be all the rage in today's game. How times have changed. In the early to mid-1980s, as the sport began to be broken down into areas of specialization, it became clear that one person could not handle all of the roles and responsibilities that came with coaching a hockey team. By the mid-1980s, the head coach was joined on the bench by one assistant coach in charge of special teams or line matchups and an assistant in the booth or the stands in charge of making adjustments to strategy. Today, NHL teams have any number of assistants who oversee everything from goaltending to video replay.

Healthy scratch

Becoming a healthy scratch is a surefire sign that your coach is not thrilled with your play. If a player is a healthy scratch then he or she has been left off the game-day roster despite the fact that they are perfectly healthy and able to participate. Deciding who will be a healthy scratch is a game-day decision made by the head coach and although healthy scratches are not in uniform they are expected to be in attendance at the game.

Helmet / lid

A hockey helmet is a hard plastic covering for the head to protect it from injury. While minor hockey in Canada has embraced the idea of its players wearing helmets en masse for over forty years now, the National Hockey League has not been so quick in making the use of helmets mandatory.

Grandfather clause: When the NHL made helmets mandatory for its players, the rule stipulated that any NHL player who played in the league before or during 1979 did not have to wear a helmet. This rule, known as a grandfather clause, allowed players like Rod Langway and Brad Marsh to play without a lid well into the 1990s. The last player to play without a helmet was Craig MacTavish, who retired in 1996.

Hit the links

Hitting the links means to trade in your hockey stick and skates for a set of golf clubs and shoes. If you are a member of a playoff team and are about to "hit the links" then your hockey season has ended and your golf season is about to begin.

Super Mario: Hockey and golf seem to go hand in hand and many hockey players are exceptional golfers. Even during his career, many wondered if Mario Lemieux would take up professional golf after he hung up his skates. Lemieux has played in a number of high-profile golf tournaments including his own tournament, the Mellon Mario Lemieux Celebrity Invitational.

Hobey Baker award

This prestigious award is given annually to the most valuable American college hockey player. Baker, a Pennsylvania native, was an all-around athlete who excelled in baseball, football, and of course, hockey and was deemed by many to be the best American hockey player never to play in the NHL. Despite not having suited up for a single game in the NHL, Baker was inducted into its hall of fame in 1945.

Baker's half dozen: The following NHL stars have all been Hobey Baker Award winners: Ryan Miller (Michigan State), Chris

Drury (Boston), Paul Kariya (Maine), Brendan Morrison (Michigan), Jordan Leopold (Minnesota), Neal Broten (Minnesota).

Hockey clichés

Step right up and pick one. How about "it's do or die" or perhaps "there's no tomorrow." Unfortunately, hockey clichés have become a staple of the post-game interview, although once in a while a Ken Dryden, Brendan Shanahan, or Brett Hull comes along, discards the script, and refreshingly, speaks from the heart.

Hockey mom

Take a trip to your local hockey arena some cold winter morning at six o'clock and look up in the rafters for the lady drinking the steaming hot cup of coffee yelling encouragement to all the kids on the ice. You've just spotted the backbone behind every successful minor hockey system in the world—the hockey mom. The tireless efforts of hockey moms across Canada were recognized when the Canadian Hockey Mom Award was presented for the first time during the 2007 Memorial Cup tournament in Vancouver.

Hockey movie

Forget *Titanic* or *Citizen Kane*. For diehard hockey fans, the only movie worth watching is a film dedicated to their favourite sport. Over the years there have been some classic hockey flicks, including *Youngblood* starring Rob Lowe; *Miracle*, documenting the amazing run by Team USA at the 1980 Olympics in Lake Placid; and of course, everyone's favourite hockey movie, *Slapshot*, starring the incomparable Paul Newman.

Miracle: Do you believe in miracles? This was the question posed by commentator Al Michaels as the clock wound down on the most spectacular upset in international hockey. On Friday, February 22, 1980, Team USA, made up of mostly untested university players, took on the "Big Red Russian Machine" in a game that would essentially determine the gold medal winner at the 1980 Lake Placid Olympic Winter Games.

Despite being outmatched and outplayed by the great Russian squad, the Americans, behind the outstanding goaltending of Jim Craig and the brilliant coaching of Herb Brooks, hung on for an improbable 4–3 win and an easy path to a gold medal victory. It was by far the greatest hockey victory for an American team, and it spawned an interest in the sport south of the border that made the United States a legitimate international hockey power.

Hockey school

Imagine a school that featured hockey morning, noon, and night, one where rebounds, refs, and (w)risters replaced reading, (w)riting, and 'rithmetic. Hockey schools throughout North America and Europe bring young players of various levels together to help them improve their skating, shooting, stickhandling, and virtually any other aspect of the game. In the past twenty years, hockey schools have evolved to become even more specialized. Instead of integrating all of the skills into one, schools now dedicate themselves to specific skills like power skating or power shooting.

Okanagan bound: Perhaps the best hockey school in the world is situated in beautiful British Columbia. The Okanagan Hockey School has been in business for over forty years and its graduates can sound like a who's who of the National Hockey League. The school, which has programs for both male and female hockey players, also has schools in the United States and Europe.

Hockey sense

Having hockey sense means having an innate feel for the game. Some players just seem to have that ability to know what play to make and when to make it.

The Hockey Song

If Stompin' Tom Connors says that hockey is the best game he can name, I am not about to argue with the living legend of country music. The song, the closest thing the game has to an anthem—*Hockey Night in Canada* theme not withstanding—is heard on a nightly basis at NHL rinks. Millions of Americans were introduced to the foot tapping ditty during Stompin' Tom's appearance on *Late Night with Conan O'Brien* in 2004.

Hockeytown

Hockeytown is the nickname given to the city of Detroit. While there is absolutely no doubt that the motor city loves its Red Wings, and the game of hockey is indeed thriving in Michigan's largest city, I think there are some other NHL cities—six in Canada for sure—that might dispute Detroit's claim.

Hockeyville: Hockeytown is not to be confused with Hockeyville. Salmon River, Nova Scotia, was the first winner of the Hockeyville contest run by the CBC and Kraft Canada. The contest, which will soon be in its third season, allows communities across Canada to compete for the title of Hockeyville and for a number of wonderful prizes that go along with it.

Hoist the Cup

To hoist the Cup means quite simply to raise the Stanley Cup up over your head after winning the holy grail of hockey. The first one to do this is always the captain of the Stanley Cup-winning team, who is awarded the Cup by the commissioner for the obligatory lap around the ice with the Cup held high.

Home opener

A team's first regular season game at home is called the home opener.

Homer

If a referee is thought to be giving the home team preferential treatment, then he or she is referred to as a "homer".

Hooking

If you use your stick to impede an opponent's progress by wrapping it around their body, then you are guilty of hooking. This is a minor offence that will get you two minutes in the sin bin.

Hurley

Although the origins of the game are still in dispute, many believe that hockey evolved from the sport of hurley. Although the sport, which uses a ball and stick and is played on grass, has European origins, it is widely believed to have been played in Canada in the early 1800s.

I

Icing

If you shoot the puck from your side of the red line into the opposing zone and past the goal line without your opponent being able to touch it, then you are guilty of icing the puck. Once your opponent eventually catches up to the puck and touches it, the linesmen will stop play and the faceoff will come all the way back into your own zone. Icing is nullified if the puck goes through the crease, is touched by the opposing goalie, is shot while your team is already shorthanded, or if either you or a teammate is able to touch the puck before an opponent can.

Touch icing: One of the hottest debates in the game today centres around the way icing is called by the officials. Playing with no-touch icing simply means that icing will be called by the officials automatically once the puck crosses the opposing goal line. At present, in the NHL, a defender needs to touch the puck in order for icing to be called and it has been argued that this leads to devastating injuries. Perhaps the most gruesome happened to Washington Capital Pat Peake. In 1996, Peake was an up-and-coming star on the Caps roster when he got badly injured trying to retrieve the puck for an icing call. Peake never recovered from his injuries and his NHL career was unjustly cut short.

IIHF

The International Ice Hockey Federation is the governing body that oversees such high-profile hockey tournaments as the World Hockey Championship and the Olympic hockey tournament. The IIHF is based in Switzerland and the current head of the federation is René Fasel.

No place to go but up: As with most sporting federations, the IIHF has rankings for both men's and women's national teams. Canada, Sweden, and Finland are at or near the top of both the men's and women's rankings. But who is last, you ask? Mongolia is the last-ranked nation in terms of men's hockey, while Turkey is bringing up the rear in the women's category.

Illegal curve

Hockey equipment is governed by a number of regulations and one of the more interesting and controversial is the rule concerning the curve of a hockey stick blade. In 2005–2006, the NHL modified the rule, allowing a three-quarter inch curve on stick blades, an increase from the previous regulation of one-half inch.

If a player is suspected of playing with an illegal stick, a stick measurement is used to determine the width of the curve. Officials will give a two-minute minor penalty to the guilty party and his or her stick will be confiscated if, in fact, the stick's curve is too large.

Merci beaucoup, Marty: In 1993, two unlikely combatants squared off for the Stanley Cup. The Los Angeles Kings and Montreal Canadiens fought their way to the final after sub-par regular seasons. The Kings were about to return to Los Angeles having won both of the first two games at the Forum when Marty McSorley was caught with an illegal curve with only minutes left to play in game two and the Kings up by one. The Canadiens tied the game with an extra attacker and won the game in OT on the strength of a seeing-eye shot by defenceman Eric Desjardins. The Canadiens went on to win the game and would take the final three games for the Cup victory.

Initiation

Initiation is a ritual that hockey teams use to welcome rookies or new additions to the squad. Initiations in leagues across North America have been increasingly under the spotlight over the last couple of decades for promoting activities that have been deemed inappropriate, demeaning, and in some cases downright dangerous.

In the system / prospects

Check out any NHL team website and you'll see a section dedicated to players who will eventually become the bedrock of the franchise. Most prospects will be those young, talented North American and European lads drafted from the various junior hockey leagues, although many can also be acquired through free agency or even as walk-ons.

J

Jake the snake

Some players seek greatness, others have greatness bestowed upon them. Jacques Plante, better known to some as Jake the Snake, never sought the spotlight, but whether it be through his play or his antics, he always seemed to be the centre of attention. Plante, the man responsible for introducing the goalie mask to the masses, was also a well-known author and talented craftsman. Plante was also an innovator in other ways, becoming the first goalie to stray from his net and regularly play the puck.

Jam

When a player has jam, it means that he or she has a mean streak and is not afraid to play physically.

Jockstrap

What do a Visa card and a jockstrap have in common? Hockey players never leave home without them. The jockstrap is the all-important athletic supporter or cup, a piece of hard plastic enclosed in an elastic band that players count on to serve and protect.

Juiced

A player using performance-enhancing drugs, specifically anabolic steroids, is said to be juiced. Fortunately, the sport of professional hockey has very few documented cases of its players abusing performance-enhancing drugs in order to elevate their game.

Pound for pound: One of the more interesting rivalries in hockey is taking place off the ice. Dick Pound, president of the World Anti-Doping Agency (WADA) and former member of the International Olympic Committee, has stated that he feels a high percentage of professional hockey players use performance-enhancing drugs, while Don Cherry vehemently disagrees with Mr. Pound's assertions.

Jumbotron

Sometimes the Jumbotron is almost as exciting as the game itself. The Jumbotron is the large video screen that sits high above ice level encouraging patrons to clap or make noise, replays highlights, displays cool graphics, and in general, keeps the fans entertained.

K

Kick save

A kick save at its most basic is simply stopping the puck by using a pad in a kicking motion, but a closer look shows that the kick save is a much more deliberate act. Keepers love to use a kick save because it helps them divert the puck to the corner or some other area of the rink that is less dangerous. The kick save is all about timing and keepers who can master the kick save help themselves immeasurably.

KLM line

Europe has produced some sensational hockey lines, including the Tres Kroner unit from Sweden, and Finland's awesome trio of Saku Koivu, Teemu Selanne, and Jari Kurri, who were simply sensational at the Nagano Olympics in 1998, but the forward grouping that was without peer was the KLM line on the Soviet Union's Red Army team.

Vladimir Krutov, Igor Larionov, and Sergei Makarov were unstoppable during their years on the Soviet Union's Olympic and world championships representative. The KLM line was magical to watch as they methodically picked apart defenders with their skill and finesse. All three forwards would eventually end up in the NHL with Larionov picking up three Stanley Cup rings with the Red Wings.

Knee-on-knee

Next to checking from behind, the most dangerous play in hockey is the "knee-on-knee" collision. A knee-on-knee hit occurs when one player sticks out his knee to impede the progress of an opponent, only to catch that player's knee with his own, sending the opponent crashing to the ice in immense pain and probably knocking him out of action for a game or two.

Knee on Neely: Cam Neely was a prototypical power forward and one of the best big men of his day. The Boston Bruin forward was in the prime of his career when he was felled by the most famous knee-on-knee incident in NHL history. Ulf Samuelsson was a tough and sometimes dirty defender with the Pittsburgh Penguins when they hooked up with the Bruins in the 1991 Eastern Conference semifinal. Early in the series, Samuelsson slammed his knee into Neely's, felling the Bruins' forward and rendering him ineffective for the rest of the series. Neely would never again be the same player and retired from the Bruins in 1996.

Knuckler

A knuckler often gives a goalie nightmares. The knuckler is a type of shot that results from the shooter only getting a piece of the puck with their blade, so that instead of sending a hard, straight shot to the net, the puck floats and flutters in different directions.

L

Lady Byng Award

If I told you that Dave "The Hammer" Schultz or Chris "Knuckles" Nilan had never won the Lady Byng Award but that Paul Kariya and Ron Francis had, do you think you could guess what this trophy represents? Lady Byng, to some better known as Marie Evelyn Moreton (1870–1949), lent her name to the NHL award that is bestowed upon the player who displays the best combination of skill and gentlemanly play in a particular season.

Last minute of play in the period

In baseball they have the seventh-inning stretch, in football they have the two-minute warning, and in hockey we mark the end of a period with an off-ice official making an announcement that there is only one minute remaining in the stanza.

Left wing lock

The left wing lock is a defensive system quite similar to the neutral zone trap. In essence, the left wing lock demands that the left winger join his team's defensive pairing on the blue line as the puck-carrying opponents approach their zone. The left wing lock is designed to do two very important things. First, by implementing the left wing lock strategy, the defensive team ensures it has enough players to account for the other team's three forwards in the defensive zone. In addition, because the opposing team has no point of entry to the zone, it forces the opposition to dump the puck in and chase it in order to regain possession—a style with which some clubs are not very comfortable.

The Legion of doom

Big, nasty, and talented, the "legion of doom" was the most dominant line of the 1990s and their numbers spoke to how powerful a forward unit they were. From 1995 through the end of the 1997 season, Philadelphia's top line of Eric Lindros, Mikael Renberg, and John LeClair scored over one hundred goals in each of the three campaigns while amassing over two hundred points in the 1995–1996 and 1996–1997 season.

Many hockey observers wonder when it was exactly that Eric Lindros stopped being the most dominant player in the league and instead became an underachieving *persona non grata* in Philadelphia. My belief is that it was the day the Flyers shipped Renberg to the Tampa Bay Lightning in exchange for Chris Gratton. The Flyers never challenged for a Stanley Cup title again and Lindros was eventually run out of Philadelphia.

Light the lamp

To light the lamp means to have scored a goal.

Lockout

Although there had been lockouts before the 1994–1995 season, it was during that year's lockout that fans quickly realized such actions would now become a permanent part of the game. A lockout occurs when NHL hockey club owners shut down play until a contractual agreement is reached between the league and its players. The first prolonged lockout occurred at the beginning of the 1994 season and did not get resolved until January of 1995, while the latest lockout forced the cancellation of the entire 2004–2005 season.

Silver lining: As with most things, though, a number of positives emerged from this very dark period in league history. The unexpected respite in 2004–2005 gave the league and its players time to address two of its most vexing problems—sky-rocketing salaries and a lack of offence in the game. A salary cap was introduced in order to address the first problem, while the introduction of a number of rule changes and a new commitment to enforce established rules gave some encouragement that stifling defensive schemes and strategies were now a thing of the past.

Long bomb

A phrase used more often in football than hockey, a long bomb in hockey occurs when a player in the defensive zone tries to hit a teammate with a long pass.

Lost an edge

As with skiers, hockey players can lose an edge and find themselves falling hard to the ice. Losing an edge is usually the result of putting too much pressure on the outside of the skate blades, or in some cases is the result of shoddy skate sharpening.

Lower body / upper body injury

And now the award for the most overused term in the NHL. National Hockey League teams are notorious for keeping injury reports closely guarded, especially during the playoffs, and you can take it to the bank that their public account of injuries will almost always include one or both of these very ambiguous medical terms.

Lucky loonie

In 2002, Canadian icemakers, responsible for making and sustaining the ice at the Salt Lake City Olympic Winter Games, placed a loonie under the centre ice dot as a good luck charm for Team Canada. Apparently they knew what they were doing, as Canada defeated Team USA for its first gold medal in hockey in fifty years.

M

Man on

Hockey coaches are constantly reminding their players that they need to protect teammates when they are out on the ice. Yelling "man on" when an opponent is chasing down an unsuspecting teammate is one very important way to do that. When a defender or forward is retrieving a puck and is unaware that the enemy is bearing down in pursuit, then the bench or players on the ice will yell "man on" to make him or her aware of the urgency of the situation.

Memorabilia

Memorabilia can consist of things like hockey cards, vintage jerseys, or personalized autographs—virtually anything that has value, sentimental or otherwise.

Mercy rule

When a game is called off because one team is beating the other too badly, we say that the game was ended by the mercy rule. The goal differential needed to introduce this rule varies from league to league, but normally it is either seven or ten goals.

Mickey Mouse franchise

You can count on one hand the number of times the media savvy Wayne Gretzky has said something to the press he later regretted, but you can count this comment he made during the 1983–84 season among them. After a game in which Gretzky and the Oilers buried the New Jersey Devils 13–4, number 99 basically called out New Jersey, describing the franchise as a "Mickey Mouse organization" that needed to put a better product on the ice. Despite the comment being an accurate assessment at the time, Gretzky later admitted it had gone too far.

Miracle on Manchester

Perhaps the greatest comeback in playoff history belongs to the Los Angeles Kings on April 10, 1982. Down 5–0 to the vaunted Edmonton Oilers and with only twenty minutes to play, things looked so bleak for the Kings that even their owner, Dr. Jerry Buss, left the building. Cue the comeback. The Kings scored six consecutive goals, including the OT winner by Daryl Evans, and stunned Edmonton 6–5. The Kings would go on to win the series and force Gretzky and the Oilers to wait one more year before reaching the finals.

Mitts

If a player has a great pair of mitts, that means he or she has superb puck-handling ability and excels at tipping pucks or making touch passes.

Motor

There's fast skaters and then there's players who can really motor. We use the term "motor" to describe players who seem to have a fifth gear they can turn on when they want. In the past decade or so, professional skating schools and camps designed specifically to improve one's skating ability have been popping up all over North America and Europe.

N

National Hockey League

Founded in 1917, the NHL is the most famous and prestigious of hockey's professional leagues. As of 2007, the league is comprised of thirty teams that play exhibition games, a regular season, and a playoff post-season to determine a champion. The Montreal Canadiens are the most successful franchise with twenty-four Stanley Cup championships to its name, while Toronto and Detroit are next with thirteen and ten Cups, respectively.

Hockey night in Moscow: It has long been felt that the NHL would someday expand to Europe. The rumours are growing ever louder that by the next decade, the National Hockey League will have teams established across the ocean that will battle the North American clubs for Lord Stanley's mug.

Net

The hockey net consists of a crossbar, two posts, and mesh, and players are constantly trying to get pucks in there. The goalie's job is to make sure that nary a puck makes its way into the net while the game is on. Perhaps the only significant change to the net has occurred with the introduction of a megg-net system that relies on magnets to keep the net in place. These nets allow for some contact, but will dislodge under any serious force, thus making them safer for any player who comes crashing toward the net at high speed.

Neutral zone

The area between the two blue lines that contains the red line and centre-ice region as well as a number of faceoff dots is the neutral zone. With the introduction of the neutral zone trap over the last decade, play in the neutral zone has taken on much greater importance than perhaps was the case in the past. Many teams, especially the New Jersey Devils, have perfected the art of clogging up the neutral zone, pouncing on turnovers, and creating offensive opportunities on the counterattack.

No goal

A "no goal" is simply a goal that has been disallowed. There are a multitude of reasons why a goal may be disallowed, including if the puck has been kicked in, has crossed the line after the net was dislodged, or has been scored while the goalkeeper was being interfered with. With the advent of video replay, the number of goals disallowed has increased in the past number of years. If a referee deems that a "no goal" call is the correct one, he or she will wave their arms as a sign that the play is dead.

Sabre rattling?: Don Cherry warned us, and his words became prophetic in June of 1999. Cherry had been telling anyone who would listen that the NHL's moronic rule that goals would be disallowed if any part of an opposing player's skate was in the crease would someday come back to haunt them. He was right.

In the final game of the 1999 Stanley Cup series between the Dallas Stars and the Buffalo Sabres, the Stars' Brett Hull scored a goal while his skate was clearly in the crease. While the Dallas players and coaches were celebrating on the ice, the Sabres were livid over the non-call and demanding a video replay. What should have been a no-goal call was instead allowed to stand and the NHL was left having to explain its decision. Mercifully, the rule was put down after the embarrassing episode and the Sabres were left to wonder, "What if?"

Non-contact hockey

Not all hockey has physical contact. There are various minor hockey and adult leagues that have banned checking and hard physical play from its associations. Women's hockey also successfully straddles the line between contact and no contact. The rules that govern women's hockey are the same as for men, except that technically there is no body checking allowed in the women's game.

Norris Trophy

The James Norris Trophy, as it is traditionally called, is awarded to the best defenceman in the National Hockey League. The trophy is named after James Norris, the Detroit Red Wings owner from 1932 to 1952.

Eight is enough: Bobby Orr would win eight consecutive Norris Trophies from 1968 to 1975.

Nosebleed section

The nosebleed section of an arena describes the seats located very high up in the stands where the sightlines are usually poor and the players can resemble ants at a picnic. One positive thing about the nosebleed sections is that the price is usually right, and considering the current price of the tickets, it may be the only ticket average fans can handle.

Novice / atom / peewee / bantam / midget

These are some of the age divisions for minor hockey teams across North America. Novice is for players seven and eight years old, atom for players nine and ten, peewee for players eleven and twelve, bantam for players thirteen and fourteen, and midget for players fifteen and sixteen.

O

The Office

The office is the area directly behind the net that Wayne Gretzky made famous. During his career, Gretzky would set up in his "office" and dare defenders to rush him and try to take the puck from him. In essence number 99 was offering opposing defenders a no-win situation. If they rushed him he would feather a pass to the open teammate for a great scoring opportunity, but if they left him alone he would work his way out to the front of the net for a scoring chance or a wrap around.

The Great One: If anyone ever wants to question how thoroughly dominating "The Great One" was during his time in the NHL, give them this stat: if you used only Wayne Gretzky's assist total, he'd still lead the NHL in total career points!

Off-setting penalties

If a referee deems that two players are guilty of an infraction—not necessarily the same one—at the same time, then off-setting penalties may be called which allows the teams to resume play with the same number of skaters per side. In other words, off-setting penalties means both teams are allowed to keep the same number of players on the ice as there were before the penalties.

Offside

The offside rule in hockey can get complicated, but it basically states that the puck must enter your opponent's zone before a player can. If a player enters the zone before the puck or if a player is already inside the zone before the puck enters then that is an offside infraction and the linesman is instructed to stop play. In some cases, and at the discretion of the on-ice officials, a player trapped in the zone may come out of the zone while the puck is being shot in and the play will be allowed to continue.

There are also different scenarios concerning where the puck will be dropped after an offside call has been made. If an official deems the offside to be intentional, then the puck will be dropped in the offending team's zone. If the offside is deemed unintentional, then the faceoff will take place in the neutral zone.

Most famous offside call: The most famous offside call was the one that wasn't made. Generally blown offside calls are neither controversial nor memorable, but in the deciding game of the 1980 Stanley Cup final between the Flyers and the Islanders, a blown offside may have secured New York's Stanley Cup win. In the first period of the deciding game in New York, Islanders rookie Duane Sutter was the beneficiary of a missed offside call by an official. The Islanders scored on the play, and the goal put the Isles up by two. They would eventually win the game and the Cup on Bob Nystrom's overtime winner.

OHL

The Ontario Hockey League is a Tier I junior hockey league with teams in Ontario and the United States. The Ontario Hockey League was established in 1934 and is one of three junior hockey leagues which comprise the Canadian Hockey League. Teams from the OHL compete for the Memorial Cup and representatives from the circuit have won a record thirty-four national championships.

Gateway to the pros: The Sault Ste. Marie Greyhounds have sent 345 of its graduates to the NHL—the most of any team in the Ontario Hockey League.

Old-time hockey

A term that can be used to describe getting back to basics or returning to fundamentals. It is also sometimes used to describe a rougher or more belligerent style of hockey.

Olympic-sized ice

Not all ice surfaces are created equal. The National Hockey League and the International Ice Hockey Federation, which oversees the Olympic hockey tournament, have vastly different regulations when it comes to the dimensions of their ice surface.

NHL rules state that the dimensions of the ice surface will be 85 feet by 200 feet, while the IIHF states that its ice surface will be 98 feet, 5 inches by 196 feet, 10 inches. Although there are arguments for and against the Olympic-sized ice surface, it is fair to say that the larger ice surface impedes the checking game and makes the match seem almost listless at certain junctures.

One-piece

No decade may have brought more profound change to the game than the 1980s. One of the more drastic evolutions occurred with the hockey stick. In the late 1980s the aluminum stick was brought to the masses and it virtually spelled the end of the wooden hockey stick.

Once Wayne Gretzky went from his wooden Titan stick to a new aluminum Easton stick, it was just a matter of time before every kid in North America made the switch. The aluminum stick has now given way to the composite one-piece hockey stick, and it, too, will probably be archaic in a few short years.

One-timer

When a shooter can accept a pass and wrist, slap, or snap a shot without having to stop the puck.

On-ice officials

These include the referee(s) and linesmen and they have very different, yet equally important duties. The referee is normally in charge of enforcing the rules, declaring goals, and promoting an atmosphere where the skill, finesse, and power of the game can be showcased. It is generally agreed that a referee is doing a good job if he or she can maintain a presence on the ice without becoming the focal point of the match. The referee will administer the opening faceoff and all of those following a goal, and can be easily recognized by the red or orange armband he or she is wearing.

The linesmen's responsibilities include dropping the puck on the vast majority of faceoffs, stopping the play for icings and offsides, and breaking up scuffles and fights that may take place before, during, or after play has begun. In recent years the role of the linesmen has expanded, and they, too, can now call infractions, including high-sticking and too many men on the ice.

On the clock

This term is heard a lot during the NHL's entry draft. Every club gets five minutes from the pick previous before they must make their selection. As soon as the previous team is finished making their pick, a clock begins to count down to the next pick, hence the expression "on the clock."

Original Six

The Original Six refers to the NHL's founding franchises that are still in existence today: Boston Bruins, Chicago Blackhawks, Detroit Red Wings, Montreal Canadiens, New York Rangers, Toronto Maple Leafs.

Match: Can you match the original six team on the left with its current arena? *Answer on page 121.*

a) Montreal Canadiens	1) United Center
b) Toronto Maple Leafs	2) Bell Centre
c) Chicago Blackhawks	3) Madison Square Garden
d) New York Rangers	4) Joe Louis Arena
e) Detroit Red Wings	5) TD Banknorth Garden
f) Boston Bruins	6) Air Canada Centre

Overtime

Overtime is the extra period(s) of hockey that needs to be played in order to decide a winner. Unlike regulation time, the team to score the first goal scored in OT is declared the victor.

Favourite OT moment: Want to get a lively discussion going among hockey fans? Ask them to recall their favourite OT moment. Younger fans might recall Brett Hull's controversial Cup winner in double OT of game six of the 1999 final against the Sabres or Jason Arnott's double OT Cup winner the following year for the Devils. For older fans, their moment might be Bobby Nystrom's sensational Cup winning tip-in against the Flyers in 1980, or Bobby Orr's sensational extra session Cup winner for the Bruins against the Blues in 1970.

Own goal

A term the sport of hockey has borrowed from soccer. If you put a puck into your own net, it counts and it is referred to as an "own goal."

P

Pad save

A goalie who uses his or her pads to stop a direct or indirect shot on goal is said to have made a "pad save."

Paddle

This term is exclusive to the goalkeeper. If you take a close look at a goaltender's stick, you'll notice that the portion just above the blade is quite wide. That portion of the stick is called the paddle. The paddle has become very important to goalies, who often lay the paddle flat on the ice as an effective tool to stop any low shots.

Penalty killer

The penalty killer has become a hockey specialist. More often than not, hockey coaches look for players with great "hockey sense" to put on the penalty kill. Killing a penalty has become an art form, and knowing the intricacies of playing the box or diamond formations will get you extra playing time on this special team's unit.

Pepper pot

Rankin Inlet's Jordin Tootoo is one of hockey's most prominent pepper pots today. Pepper pots like to stir things up and create chaos on the ice while giving their team a much-needed shot of energy and adrenaline. More often than not, these men and women are not the biggest players on the ice, but they prefer to be judged on the size of their heart as opposed to the size of their body.

Period

Depending on whether you are playing local tournaments, college or international hockey, or even professional hockey, periods can last from ten to twenty minutes of running or stop time. In the pro game, regular season games will see three twenty-minute, stop-time periods followed by a five-minute overtime, if necessary, and a shootout, if necessary. In the playoffs, the NHL retains the three twenty-minute stop periods, but the extra periods are twenty minutes in duration until someone scores and is declared a winner.

Pest

When opponents nickname you "The Rat," you know you're getting under their skin. The Rat, of course, was Flyer, Oiler, and Bruin great

Kenny Linseman, and he was a card-carrying member of the super-pest fraternity that also includes Flames great Theo Fleury and current New York Ranger instigator Sean Avery.

Playing the man

Playing the man and not the puck is a fundamental skill that young players are taught very early. All players, but especially defenders, are reminded time and time again to focus on the movements of the opposing player and not on the movements of the puck. Coaches will tell you that if you can zero in on the chest of your opponent and take them out of the play, while resisting the temptation to follow the puck, you will lose far fewer one-on-one battles.

Playoff beard

The sales of razor blades slump drastically during the NHL playoffs, when players do not shave until they've been eliminated from the post-season or have captured the Cup. The playoff beard is a long-established tradition in the sport of hockey. Other team playoff superstitions may come and go but the playoff beard is a post-season staple.

Plumbers / utility players

These are the players who have more heart than talent and more guts than grace. Plumbers are willing to go places the stars are unwilling to go and to do things the stars are unwilling to do, all for the sake of making the cut and staking out their place on the roster. The plumbers on a hockey team play no more than five or six minutes a game and are expected to be Jacks (or Jackies if you will) of all trades.

Plus-minus

A stat that can be both deceiving and overrated, the plus-minus rating is determined by taking the difference between the number of goals a player is on the ice for when his team scores (even strength or shorthanded) minus the number of goals he or she is on for when the opposition has scored (at even strength or short-handed).

The problems with properly interpreting the plus-minus are many. For example, the statistic doesn't take into account the total minutes a player has played per game. If a player is on the ice for only two minutes a game and comes away with a zero plus-minus rating, it hardly deserves equal weight to a teammate who has been on the ice for thirty minutes a game and has earned the same rating.

Poke check

One of the brilliantly subtle skills of the game of hockey, the poke check is accomplished by using the blade of your stick to knock the puck off an opponent's stick. The poke check is all about timing and giving yourself the chance to recover defensively if the poke check fails. When the poke check is being used to perfection, the defender allows the puck-carrying opponent to come close enough so that a quick jab can jar the puck off the opponent's blade.

The key to a good poke check is the ability to recover and get back in the play quickly if the puck isn't dislodged from an opponent's stick.

Policeman

Wayne Gretzky had Dave Semenko, Steve Yzerman had Bobby Probert, and Sidney Crosby had big Georges Laraque. Every team employs that one player who will make life miserable for you if you give the team's resident superstar a hard time. None of the tough guys mentioned above threatened to win the scoring race and none received honourable mention when the Lady Byng Trophy for gentlemanly play was awarded, but their value to their teams is unquestioned.

Post-concussion syndrome

Head injuries are becoming a grave concern for the NHL. Post-concussion syndrome, or PCS as it is widely known in hockey circles, describes the group of side effects that linger after the initial diagnosis of a concussion has been made. These maladies, which can include dizziness and headaches, can stay with a concussed athlete for months or even years.

Nagano nightmare: The 1998 Winter Olympics in Nagano, Japan, may have been Canada's lowest moment in international hockey after our country failed to win a medal despite being considered a heavy favourite to win the tournament. Our fate may have been sealed a few weeks before the Olympics when Chicago's Gary Suter viciously slammed his stick into Paul Kariya's head, felling the Anaheim star and putting him out of action with a concussion. Kariya was playing sensational hockey at the time and had gained valuable Olympic experience in Norway four years earlier. His forced departure from Team Canada was a major factor in stopping our quest for gold.

Power forward

There are forwards and then there are power forwards. Unlike the better-known finesse forwards like Gretzky, Kariya, and Lafleur, NHL power forwards like Joe Thornton, Keith Tkachuk, and former Leaf great Wendel Clark went through defenders as opposed to going around them. As with all things related to the NHL, the power forward has changed over the decades. While Gordie Howe, who was just six feet tall and weighed a little over two hundred pounds, was defining the position in the 1950s and 1960s, Thornton and Tkachuk are using their imposing size—six-foot-four, two hundred pounds and six-foot-two, two hundred and twenty pounds, respectively—and skill to dominate today's game.

Pre-game warm-up

Teams usually have fifteen minutes or so before the game officially begins to warm-up or prepare themselves for the encounter. Teams take advantage of this time to take shots on the goalkeeper, practise three-on-two situations, test skates, sticks, and other equipment, and stretch.

Pre-season / regular season / post-season

For most teams the hockey season can be broken into three distinct parts. The pre-season consists of a dozen or so games that allow players to get their timing and endurance back and allow for coaches to make roster and team strategy decisions. The regular season is typically the longest of the three parts and in the case of NHL, lasts for exactly eighty two games. The post-season is better known as the playoffs and can consist of a either a tournament-style championship, as in the NCAA, or a series-style post-season like in the NHL.

Presidents' Trophy

This trophy is awarded annually to the NHL team that garners the most regular season points.

Puck hog

The puck hog is usually referred to as any player who selfishly keeps the puck and doesn't pass it to a teammate. The puck hog would seemingly rather have the puck stolen by an opponent than make a timely pass or dump the puck into the offensive zone. Puck hogs quickly draw the ire of teammates and coaches alike and generally are not great team players, except...

Boss hog: Wayne Gretzky once said that his philosophy was that the puck was his and if you wanted to touch it, you should go get your own—spoken like a true puck hog. The Great One is a perfect example of how being a puck hog is not always a negative. Gretzky's phenomenal assist total proved that special players who demand the puck can also be tremendously effective playmakers.

Pylon

The pylon can be a helpful, little orange object used by almost every coach to augment their skating and stickhandling drills. The second definition is not so flattering. A pylon in hockey can also describe the hapless athlete who is devoid of any hockey talent and whose hockey-playing acumen draws a comparison to a stationary piece of plastic.

Q

QMJHL

The Quebec Major Junior Hockey League is a Tier I junior hockey league in Canada and along with the OHL and the WHL operate under the umbrella of the Canadian Hockey League. The "Q," as it is affectionately known, is made up of teams from Quebec, all of the Atlantic provinces, and the state of Maine.

Quarterback

In the NFL, where this term is often used, any list of great contemporary quarterbacks must include Brett Favre, Tom Brady, and Peyton Manning. In the NHL, however, quarterbacks go by the name of Lidstrom, Redden, and the Conn Smythe–winning Scott Niedermayer.

The role of the quarterback in hockey is to set up the power play so that goal scorers receive a tape-to-tape pass for a quick one-timer.

Whether you're a pro team or a minor hockey formation special teams is a bigger key to wining hockey games than it has ever been and a power play quarterback who has the ability to generate offence from the defence position is an absolute must.

Quick whistle

This term is used to describe a play that has been called dead by an official when the puck is clearly still in play. Because referees must blow their whistle when they lose sight of the puck, there are times, unfortunately, when they whistle the play dead prematurely.

R

Ragging the puck

Ragging the puck is similar to the game "keep away." A player uses his stickhandling ability to keep the puck away from opposing players. Most often, this tactic is used to kill a penalty or to waste time on the clock to protect a lead.

Referee crease

You may not have noticed, but if you take a close look at the ice surface the next time you are watching a hockey game, you'll spot a small semicircle by the timekeeper's box that is an oasis for the on-ice officials. When officials want to get together for a private conversation or consultation, they simply head to their private area and players are not allowed to encroach upon them here.

Rental

When a team trades for a player knowing full well that the player will be heading elsewhere at the end of the season, then that player is called a rental. In most cases a rental player is acquired on or near the trading deadline.

Restricted / unrestricted free agent

Free agency may be the best thing to ever happen to professional athletes, not only in hockey, but in every professional sport which features it. Free agency allows players to determine where they want to play, for how much money, and for how long. Restricted free agency, which states that a player can sign with a franchise pending certain conditions, is not as attractive to an athlete as unrestricted free agency.

Retaliation penalty

Often referees will penalize an act of retaliation and not the initial check or contact. A retaliation penalty is often born out of frustration or bruised ego and is seen as a selfish penalty. Coaches do not have a lot of patience with hockey players who put themselves ahead of the team and force their side to play short-handed for the sake of a little revenge.

Retired numbers

One way a franchise can honour or recognize an athlete is to retire that player's number. Normally the player is recognized during a pre-game ceremony where their jersey is raised to the rafters never to be worn by any players on that team again.

? **Trivia:** Only one jersey number has been retired by every single NHL club. Can you guess which number will never again be worn in the National Hockey League? *Answer on page 121.*

Riding the pine

If you're playing less than five minutes per game, then you really are riding the pine. The good news is that you are still in the lineup; the bad news is that the coach doesn't have much confidence in you.

Ringette

Ringette is a team sport played on an ice surface and has many similarities to the game of hockey. First introduced in Ontario in the early 1960s, ringette is a tremendously fast game played on ice with a stick and rubber ring.

Rink / arena

The venue in which hockey games are played.

The Roadrunner

"Roadrunner" is the nickname given to Yvon Cournoyer. Cournoyer, the captain of the Canadiens during their four-year-sit atop the league in the late 1970s had an incredible set of wheels, hence the Roadrunner moniker.

Robbed

To be robbed is to have been the victim of a great save.

Rob Ray rule

Rob Ray was a superbly skilled pugilist and one of few NHLers to have a rule named after him. Rob Ray was famous for having his jersey disintegrate the moment he began exchanging haymakers with a challenger. The NHL brain trust, tired of seeing Ray's naked midriff, designed a rule that made it mandatory for players to tie down their jerseys. To underscore how serious they were about having players keep their shirt on, so to speak, the NHL doled out game misconduct penalties to players who refused to obey the tie-down law.

Hands of steel and a heart of gold: Rob Ray was as mean as they came once he laced up the skates. Off the ice, though, Ray was a very generous man and his generosity was rewarded in 1999 when he was awarded the King Clancy Memorial Trophy for humanitarian contributions.

Rock 'em sock 'em

Rock 'em sock 'em hockey is a brand of hockey highlighted by hard hitting, rough play, plenty of fisticuffs, and close checking. A best-selling series of videos put together by hockey commentator Don "Grapes" Cherry is also called "Rock 'Em Sock 'Em Hockey."

Roller hockey

Roller hockey is a variation of ice hockey played on an asphalt or rubber playing surface and uses Rollerblades instead of hockey skates. Roller hockey's popularity peaked in the mid-1990s when professional teams from various leagues played to packed houses across North America.

Rondelle

Rondelle is the French translation for the word "puck."

Roof daddy

A close relation to the phrase, "where Grandma hides the cookies." If you have just scored with a laser to the top corner then you've just gone "roof daddy." There is perhaps nothing prettier in hockey than the sight of a booming slapshot snapping twine just below the crossbar. If you're a fan of Mario Lemieux, you'll know where the saying, "where Grandma hides the cookies" originated. Number 66 used to love to skate in on a hapless opposing goaltender, draw him to his knees with a terrific deke, and then snap one just above the goalie's shoulder into the top shelf. Mike Lange, the creative, long-time Penguins' announcer, used to describe it as shooting "where Grandma hides the cookies."

Rout

A game will be described as a "rout" if one team is able to run up the score on the opposition, but a game can also be categorized as a rout if one team is totally dominating the game even if the score does not recognize it.

Rover

Back in the early days of the sport, the rover had an actual place in the game. Being used as a seventh player, the rover was given the mandate of cruising the ice surface with no particular limitations on where he or she could go. The rover was also given much more leeway, in terms of what their offensive and defensive roles and responsibilities were. While the position of rover may not be in existence anymore, great players like Ovechkin, Crosby, and St. Louis are still given a great deal of freedom by their coaches to seek out areas on the ice where they can use their superb talents.

S

Salary cap

This term is relatively new to hockey. In general terms, a salary cap limits a team's total salary paid out to its players. In the case of the National Hockey League, the salary cap also has a minimum salary standard, meaning that a team has a lower limit for its total salary. For the 2005–2006 hockey season, the first under the new collective agreement, the salary cap was set at $39 million per team, with each team required to spend at least $21.5 million.

Saucer

No this is not something you need to report to the FBI, nor is it material for an episode of the *X-Files*. If you've seen a saucer at a local hockey game then you've just spotted one of the more finesse-intensive plays in the game of hockey. The saucer is a pass that is made from one player to another that can be breathtaking in its precision and subtlety.

The saucer pass is a tape-to-tape effort where the distributor needs to lift the puck over a defender's stick or body to the receiver, who is usually in full stride. The pass needs to be hard enough that it can take flight as soon as it leaves the distributor's stick but soft enough that the receiver can pick it up without having to slow down or make the puck settle smoothly. Mastering the saucer pass demands superb hand-eye coordination and the ability to anticipate an opposing defender's motives.

Savardian spinerama

A term coined by the iconic Canadiens announcer Danny Gallivan to describe the patented move by the great Montreal blueliner Serge Savard. Although superstars like Bobby Orr and Denis Potvin were blessed with more natural talent than the Canadiens stalwart, no player could execute the eloquent spinerama better than number 18 of the Habs. Almost a half-dozen times a game, Savard would take the puck and skate directly at an opposing forward only to spin 180 degrees at the last second, leaving the defender behind and completely out of the play. The move was pure ballet on ice and Gallivan's use of the term made it a staple of any Canadiens broadcast.

Save percentage

Save percentage is a statistic that represents the percentage of shots on goal a goaltender stops. The stat is calculated by dividing the number of saves by the total number of shots on goal.

Score sheet

The official score sheet is a specially designed form that allows off-ice officials to account for such info as goals, assists, penalties, and shots on goal, and is turned over to the league upon completion of each game.

Screen

There is an old saying in baseball that you can't hit what you can't see. In hockey we might instead say that you can't stop what you can't see. When forwards see the puck passed back to a defenceman in the offensive zone, their first thought should be to head directly to the net and create a screen, a human wall that does not allow the goalie to see the puck. As long as they are not directly interfering with the keeper's ability to stop the puck, forwards can set up shop directly in front of the net and try to make it impossible to see the puck as it is shot.

Scrimmage

A scrimmage is used to describe a friendly game between two opposing clubs. Coaches sometimes like to use a ten- or fifteen-minute scrimmage at the end of practice to give players a feel for game-day conditions. A scrimmage is very informal and is less concerned with rules and regulations than an exhibition game or a regular season match.

Scrum

A term that has been borrowed from the sport of rugby, a scrum occurs when a number of players congregate after the whistle to push and shove and generally delay the game. The referee has the discretion to penalize players who are overly aggressive during a scrum or who prolong the scrum unnecessarily.

Selke Trophy

This trophy is presented annually to the top defensive player in the NHL. This award is relatively new having been first awarded in 1978.

High praise: Bob Gainey was the first player awarded the Selke Trophy and is the only NHLer to win it four times. In 1976 the Russian national team head coach Viktor Tikhonov called Gainey the best player in the world—high praise indeed for a defensive specialist.

The Shadow

The most underappreciated job in the sport of hockey is held by the player known only as the shadow. Shadows plant themselves firmly on the hip of the opposing team's superstar and never allows him or her out of sight. The shadow's job is quite simple: it is to make the life of their target miserable and to make sure that by hook or by crook—with the emphasis on hook—the high-flying target is kept out of the game as much as possible.

Me and my shadow: For years until they became teammates in Motown, Brett Hull's shadow was the ultra-talented Sergei Federov; Mario Lemieux's nemesis was the New York Islanders' super-pest Darius Kasparaitis; Montreal Canadiens' superstar Guy Lafleur couldn't turn around without feeling the Boston Bruins' Don Marcotte breathing down his neck. For the most part, the shadow plays in anonymity, but as the old hockey saying goes, show me a Stanley Cup champion and I'll show you a shadow who played his or her role to perfection.

Shifts

Shifts can have a couple of meanings. If someone on the bench asks "Whose shift is it?" then he or she wants to know whose line gets on the ice next. Shifts can also mean the amount of time a player or line spends on the ice. A normal shift usually lasts between forty-five seconds to a minute but it is not unusual to see a coach limit his team's shifts to twenty-five to thirty seconds in the last five to ten minutes of a game.

Shoot-in

Don Cherry swears by the shoot-in. In hockey there are two methods of entering an opponent's zone: by carrying the puck in, or by shooting the puck in. On a shoot-in as a defenceman or forward approaches the opponent's blue line, he shoots the puck deep into the zone and attempts to retrieve the puck through a forecheck.

The shoot-in is effective for a couple of reasons. First, the shoot-in forces the opponent to go the length of the ice in order to get a scoring opportunity, and second, it allows a team to physically punish the other team's players by using a forecheck.

Shootout

A hockey shootout occurs when the overtime period ends without a winner. In the NHL, three skaters are picked from each team to shoot one-on-one against the goalie. If a winner is not declared after the initial three shooters, then one player from each team will continue to shoot until a winner is declared.

Swede sensation: Arguably the greatest shootout goal ever came at the 1994 Winter Olympics in Lillehammer, Norway, when Sweden's Peter Forsberg pulled Canada's Corey Hirsch out of the net before sweeping the puck behind him for the gold-medal-winning marker.

Short-handed

Under normal circumstances a team will have five skaters and a goaltender on the ice at all times. A team can find itself short-handed, though, if it has had one or more players banished to the penalty box, or if for some reason a rash of injuries has depleted its lineup.

Shots on goal

A shot on goal is registered as such when the puck either enters the net or is saved by the keeper after being directed toward the goal by the opposing team. Shots that hit the crossbar, for example, are not considered shots on goal although there is a movement to try and change that rule. Shots on goal are determined through the judgement of a statistician assigned to each game and are considered a crucial stat by most coaches.

Sieve

A goalie who suffers from a sunburn attained from the red light continually going on behind him, he may very well be a sieve. A sieve is a nasty term used to describe a goalie who gets scored on early and often.

Red Light Racicot: André Racicot is the Rodney Dangerfield of NHL goalies—he just can't get any respect. Racicot, who was a backup for Patrick Roy in Montreal during the early 1990s, had a propensity for giving up bad goals and the patrons at the Forum were not averse to giving him the raspberries.

After one of his sub-par performances, someone tagged the nickname "Red Light Racicot" on the keeper and it stuck. André Racicot got the last laugh, however, as he sports a Stanley Cup ring from the Canadiens' 1993 finals win over Los Angeles.

Signing bonus / production bonus

Bonuses have become key features of any contract. The signing bonus is the money given to a player simply for signing a contract. The moment a player puts his or her signature on the dotted line, then the signing bonus kicks in. A production bonus, however, is determined by how much a player produces during the season. If a player gets selected to an all-star game for example, he may receive a bonus for having done so, and in some cases a player is rewarded for team successes as opposed to individual accomplishments.

Sin bin

For NHL bad boys like Tie Domi, the sin bin was a sort of home away from home. The penalty box, as it is otherwise known, is the place where you go to take a time out and think about the misdeeds you've done. Some minor infractions, like tripping an opposing player or closing your hand on the puck, require a mere two minutes or less of penalty time. More serious infractions like fighting result in the player spending five minutes in isolation, while major misdeeds, like a misconduct for complaining to the referee too aggressively, can get you ten minutes of hard time.

Sitting on a lead

Probably the worst thing a team can do is sit on a lead, and yet time after time, teams revert to this defensive posture once they've gone up by a goal or two. Sitting on a lead means to abandon any sustained fore-check and any attempt to generate scoring in exchange for staying back and trying to protect the lead. Of course, as the saying goes, the best defence is a good offence, and invariably teams that sit on a lead almost always give up the very lead they were trying to protect.

Sixth player

In some rinks the fans are actually like a sixth player. The moment players step onto the ice at the "Shark Tank" in San Jose or "The Joe" in Detroit, they feel the incredible energy emanating from the galleries. The home-ice advantage is often worth at least a goal to the hometown squad.

Fan-tastic: On April 23, 1996, the Tampa Bay Lightning set an all-time NHL attendance record as 28,183 fans packed the Thunderdome for game four of the Eastern Conference quarter-final versus Philadelphia.

Sledge hockey

Sledge hockey is a form of hockey played by athletes with disabilities. Sledge hockey is thought to have existed for approximately four decades and is fast becoming one of the marquee sports in the Paralympic Games. The sport's rules and regulations, including the size of the ice surface, are similar to those of hockey and are overseen by the IHEC (Ice Hockey Executive Committee).

Our game: The Canadian Paralympic sledge hockey team took gold in 2006 in Turin, Italy. Team Canada was outstanding in a 3–0 win against perennial sledge hockey powerhouse Team Norway.

Slew-foot

A very dangerous action that can result in a serious head injury to an opponent. The slew-foot is the action of taking the feet out from an opposing player or pushing an opposing player's skates forward from behind.

Slot

If Donald Trump were a hockey player you'd probably find him in the slot, because in the world of hockey, the slot is known as prime real estate. The slot is the area directly in front of the crease where most goals are scored from and where most of the real action takes place. Some of the greatest scorers in the game, like Brett Hull and Phil Esposito, made the slot their home away from home.

Slug

There aren't many terms less flattering to a hockey player than being called a slug. In the NHL, a slug is usually the player who makes a three-million-dollar-a-year salary but for some reason has forgotten how to hit, score, or scrap. Generally the slug disappears when the going gets tough or the stakes get high and that ultimately earns him the wrath of the hometown fans. Unfortunately for today's NHL general managers, one-way contracts usually ensure that their slugs are going to be an albatross around the team's financial neck for a while. By the way, in Ottawa, they spell slug Y–A–S–H–I–N!

Slump

A slump in hockey can affect a team, a player, or even a franchise. A team that goes through a long stretch without a win is considered to be in a slump, a skater who has had his or her scoring touch disappear is slumping, and a keeper who suddenly can't stop a beach ball is also in a slump.

Desperately seeking Stanley: Two original six hockey clubs are desperate to get their names on Lord Stanley's mug again. In fact, two of the longest Stanley Cup droughts belong to original six franchises. The Chicago Blackhawks have not won the mug since 1961 while Toronto has not had a Cup parade since 1967.

Snap shot

The snap shot is sometimes described as a compromise between the slapshot and the wrist shot. The snap shot, like the slapshot, will see the stick come off the ice, but unlike the slapper, the snap shot does not have a long windup and therefore has an element of surprise that resembles the wrister.

Sniper

The sniper is the player on your club who seems to have that innate ability to find the back of the net. While most of us need to find ourselves in the zone directly in front of the opposing goalie in order to pull the trigger, the sniper is blessed with a God-given talent to dent the twine from anywhere on the ice. Snipers can have three defenders draped all over them and their stick tied up at a seemingly impossible angle and still find a way to turn the red light on.

There was a time in the dead-puck era of the 1930s and 1940s when potting twenty goals in a season would qualify you as a sniper...not so anymore. Since the game became a scorer's paradise in the late 1960s, it takes at least one fifty-goal season on your resumé to get such consideration. Through the years there have been some incredibly gifted pure goal scorers. Mike Bossy and Jari Kurri come to mind, but the consensus is that in the offensive zone, nobody had a knack for the net like Montreal's mighty Maurice "Rocket" Richard.

Sophomore jinx

When pro athletes enter their second season, especially if they have had spectacular rookie campaigns, they are always a little leery about coming under the spell of the sophomore jinx. The sophomore jinx describes the tendency for some players to incur a substantial drop in production during the sophomore season or even worse, an injury.

Specialist

A specialist is a hockey player who garners most of his or her ice time in particular situations. The forte of a specialist may include taking faceoffs, killing penalties, playing the power play, playing on the checking line, or fighting.

Quick draw McGraw: Doug Jarvis wasn't a great scorer, he wasn't a real tough guy, nor did he get much time on the power play, but he could win a crucial faceoff with his eyes closed. Jarvis parlayed his unique calling into a long and distinguished career that spanned fifteen years and almost one thousand games.

Standing "O"

You know you've done something pretty special when you can bring twenty thousand people to their feet. A standing "O" occurs when you've brought the masses out of their chairs and have them clapping and singing in unison.

Mr. Hockey's finest moment: If you ever want to experience chills running up and down your spine, try to find a copy of the 1980 NHL All-Star game, specifically the players' introduction. For almost ten minutes, the crowd of twenty thousand plus at the Joe Louis

Arena gave number nine, Gordie Howe, a standing "O" that left everyone in the building and watching at home in tears. For Howe, it would be a fitting farewell to the city that made him famous and the game that made him a superstar.

Standing room only

When a rink is so packed that some patrons need to stand because there just aren't any seats available, then we describe the venue as being standing room only. Some buildings issue standing-room-only (or SRO) tickets for a reduced cost, since it can become very uncomfortable to stand for an entire game.

Standings

Standings document or illustrate a team's position in their particular league. Normally the standings will include a team's wins, losses, overtime losses, and ties, if applicable, and a team's point total.

Stanley Cup

The most celebrated trophy in all of sport, the Stanley Cup was donated to the game by Lord Stanley of Preston in 1892. Although the NHL was the only league vying for the trophy beginning in 1926, it wasn't until 1947 that it retained sole propriety over the holy grail.

Stanza

A stanza is another name for a period in ice hockey.

Stitched up

To be "stitched up" means to receive stitches, usually after being struck by the puck or an errant stick or skate. Of course, hockey players are infamous for their pain threshold, so normally the doctors stitch up any cuts and the player returns to the game.

The Stopper

Perhaps the greatest thing the New Jersey Devils had going for them in their three Cup victories spanning nine seasons was their goaltender. Opposing players would look down the ice and know that even if they got by the Devils' stifling defensive schemes, they still faced the prospect of facing one of the best goalies in the world, Martin Brodeur.

In baseball the stopper is the pitcher who nails down a victory for his or her club. In hockey, the stopper is the goalie who, time after time, shuts the door on opposing forwards and gives his or her team that impenetrable last line of defence.

? **Trivia:** While Marty Brodeur has always been acknowledged as the linchpin of the Devils' three Stanley Cup victories, he has never won the playoff MVP award, better known as the Conn Smythe Trophy. Who were the three Conn Smythe winners in 1995, 2000, and 2003—the years the Devils won the cup? *Answer on page 121.*

Straddle the line

To straddle the blue line means to have one skate inside the opponent's zone and one skate still in the neutral zone. The purpose of straddling the blue line is to prevent an offside call, thus allowing play to carry on.

Substitution

A substitution occurs when one player is replaced by another. A special quirk of the game of hockey is that it is the only professional game where replacements can be made while the play is actually going on ("on the fly").

Suicide pass

NHL blueliners like Dion Phaneuf and Ed Jovanovski make their living destroying opponents who are on the wrong side of one of these. The suicide pass is, of course, a feed from teammate to teammate where the receiver is put in a vulnerable position such that he or she will get smacked the second the puck is touched. If you want to get on the bad side of a teammate, keeping dishing him this type of pass on a regular basis.

The Summit Series

Quickly now, where were you the exact moment Paul Henderson slid that rebound past a sprawling Vladislav Tretiak with thirty-six seconds left in game eight of the greatest hockey series of all time?

For those of us lucky enough to remember Henderson's heroic effort, the answer is very easy—we were glued to our television sets, hoping and praying that Team Canada would have one more come-from-behind victory in their pocket. Thirty-five years after the goal that gave Canada the series victory, the Summit Series is still regarded as the greatest hockey series ever played and will forever be our nation's proudest hockey moment.

Sun Belt cities

The Sun Belt cities are the southern American locales that are not traditional hockey markets but whose growing population and influence gained them NHL franchises in the 1990s. Tampa Bay, Phoenix, and Miami are examples of Sun Belt cities with NHL franchises.

Support/outlet

Sometimes hockey players will yell "support" to each other on the ice. Supporting a teammate means being close enough to receive a pass if the teammate is in trouble or about to get checked. Similarly, an outlet is a player who becomes an option if a teammate is about to lose the puck or about to get hit.

Sweep

A sweep happens when one team defeats another in a series of games without incurring a loss. The term is used particularly for describing playoff victories where one team has won every game.

T

Tag up

In an effort to maintain the flow of the game and to eliminate whistles caused by the offside rule, the NHL instituted a tag-up rule a number of years ago that allowed players who were in an offside position to come back out of the zone and touch, or tag, the blue line before going back in to resume their efforts.

Telestrator

Have you ever wondered what the name of that nifty machine is that allows hockey analysts to create game-day images on screen? Well, that machine is called a telestrator. The telestrator, first made popular by the incomparable Howie Meeker, allowed commentators to draw over top of a moving image for further analysis of instant replay.

Tempo

Tempo is used to describe the pace of a game. Normally the tempo of the game ebbs and flows with segments that are terrifically fast and uptempo and others that seemed bogged down and excruciatingly slow. In the NHL, new rules have been established to try and make sure that the tempo of the game is more like the former and less like the latter.

Third player in

If a third player enters an altercation in progress, the player will be nailed with a "third player in" violation and an automatic game misconduct penalty.

Three-on-three (tournament)

In arenas across North America, the three-on-three tournament is quickly becoming one of the more popular ways to play the sport. The three-on-three is played with two forwards and a defenceman on the ice in addition to a goalkeeper. The rise in popularity of the three-on-three format can be attributed to its emphasis on offence and goaltending and the ability for smaller players to showcase their talent.

Three-star selection

A fan favourite, especially in Canadian cities, this grand gesture of highlighting three players of the game has been a tradition in NHL rinks for well over half a century. At the end of a match, players will be introduced as either the first, second, or third star and return to the ice surface, where they receive a standing ovation, or in the case of an opponent, tepid applause.

First, second, and third star: On March 23, 1944, after another spectacular effort against Toronto, Maurice "Rocket" Richard was honoured by being selected the first, second, and third star!

Tier II

A Tier II hockey league, or junior A league, is considered by most to be one notch below the CHL in terms of talent and prestige. Tier II hockey leagues are governed by the Canadian Junior A Hockey League, which oversees ten constituent leagues across Canada.

Tip / tip-in

Goalies will tell you that the most difficult save to make is one that involves a deflected puck or tip. The tip-in will usually confuse the goalie into moving one way while the puck is deflected in another direction, resulting in a goal.

Toe drag

The toe drag is one of the prettiest plays in hockey and one of the more difficult to master. The toe drag is a move that the player with the puck uses to force the defender into making a lunge with his stick, allowing the puck carrier to deftly pull the puck into his body and around said defender. The trick to making this bit of stickhandling wizardry work is selling the move so that the defender believes she can successfully stick-check the puck away. Once the defender has committed, the offensive player can simply roll her wrists into her mid-section by using the tip of the stick blade to corral the puck and simply sidestep the vulnerable defender, who has no chance for recovery once committed to making a lunge for the puck.

The Torpedo

In their first game of the 2002 Winter Olympics, Team Canada became the unsuspecting victims of a strategy that had been mostly under wraps for nearly three decades. Swedish hockey had been waiting to spring its new and devastating torpedo system on the international hockey world and finally did on an overwhelmed Team Canada on February 10, 2002.

The torpedo system, which has become an answer to our North American defensive trap system, cripples an opposing team's offensive scheme by smothering opposition defenders and leaving opposing forwards to fend for themselves without any support. The forwards enter the zone in pairs, leaving only one central defender to watch the front of the net. As with most sports strategies, however, the torpedo has also been shown to be fallible and has not yet gained a foothold in North American hockey.

Trade

Trades usually involve an exchange of players, draft picks, or cash between two or more hockey clubs, although past NHL transactions have also included coaches, equipment, and even a team bus. The National Hockey League has long had a trading deadline that prohibited teams from making trades after a predetermined date. NHL teams that are active at the trading deadline are usually seen as either buyers or sellers, with buyers beefing up their roster for a run at the Cup and sellers trying to rid themselves of big contracts and unwanted players.

Trade bait: The Boston Bruins were front and centre in two of the biggest deals ever made in the NHL. During the 1975–1976 season, Hall of Fame great Phil Esposito went from Boston to the Rangers along with Carol Vadnais in exchange for Brad Park, Joe Zanussi, and

Jean Ratelle, while in 2000 the Bruins shipped Norris Trophy winner Ray Bourque and forward Dave Andreychuk to Colorado in exchange for Brian Rolston, Samuel Pahlsson, Martin Grenier, and a first-round draft pick. The biggest trade of all occurred in 1988 when Wayne Gretzky, Marty McSorley, and Mike Krushelnyski were shipped to Los Angeles for Jimmy Carson, Martin Gelinas, draft picks, and cash.

Trapezoid

Aren't you glad you paid attention when your grade eleven math teacher explained what a trapezoid was? In 2005, the NHL introduced a rule that established a designated area (the trapezoid) behind the goal line where goalies could play the puck. A goalie who plays the puck behind the goal line but not in the designated trapezoid area, will be given a two-minute minor penalty. The intent of the rule is to limit the ability of goalies to come out of their net and shoot the puck out of the zone, preventing a sustained forecheck by the opposition and therefore limiting scoring opportunities.

Some hockey purists felt that the trapezoid rule, in addition to some of the others instituted after the 2004–2005 lockout, changed the game too drastically. Many felt it was a case of too much, too soon in terms of rule changes and chastised the league for fixing something that was not broken. Criticism aside, the trapezoid rule has helped encourage a sustained forecheck in the game and the new rules appear to be somewhat responsible for an increase in scoring after the lockout.

Transactions

A hockey transaction normally centres around the drafting, signing, trading, or retiring of a player or coach. It can also include injuries or suspensions.

Trapper / blocker

These are integral pieces of the goalkeeper's equipment. The trapper is what goalies use on their catching hand and is similar to a baseball glove in purpose, if not design. The blocker is used on the non-catching hand to direct pucks away from the net. The hard outer shell of the blocker allows the keeper to stop hard shots without fear of injury.

The Triple Crown line

For many hockey players in the 1970s and 1980s, having to play in Los Angeles was like being dispatched to the outer reaches of Siberia, but Marcel Dionne, Charlie Simmer, and Dave Taylor thrived on the California sunshine and formed one of the more devastating lines in the history of the game. Dionne, of course, was the straw that stirred this drink, scoring fifty or more goals six times in a Kings uniform and garnering one hundred points or more seven times during that span. Taylor and Simmer weren't exactly chopped liver either when it came to getting on the score sheet. Simmer racked up two fifty-plus-goal seasons in LA, while Taylor topped the century mark in point scoring twice.

? **Trivia:** Team Canada's 1976 team is considered by many to be the best hockey team ever assembled. In the final game of the '76 Canada Cup, Marcel Dionne and Lanny McDonald assisted on the winning OT goal by? *Answer on page 121.*

A) Bobby Orr
B) Darryl Sittler
C) Denis Potvin
D) Guy Lafleur

Trolley tracks

If you have ever had your head down looking at the puck while travelling through the trolley tracks, chances are you landed flat on your back courtesy of a hard-hitting defenceman from the opposing team. In hockey, the trolley tracks is the section of the ice between the two blue lines and between the dots that forwards love to skate into as they pick up speed going up the ice. If they aren't careful, though, the trolley tracks can soon become the devil's triangle. Just ask one of many unsuspecting NHL forwards who cruised through the trolley tracks unaware that New Jersey's Scott Stevens was about to lower the boom.

Turtle

If you are an NHL player, there is one way to guarantee that you get on "Coach's Corner," and that is to "turtle" during a fight. If there is one thing that Don Cherry cannot stomach, it is a player getting into the fetal position once he finds himself in the middle of a fracas. Cherry has called out more than a few players, including his least favourite player of all time, Claude Lemieux, for hitting the deck instead of taking one on the bugle.

Tweaked

As in "tweaked his knee" or "tweaked his elbow." This term is relatively new to hockey lingo and it is used to describe a minor injury that is not serious enough to send a player to the infirmary or the showers but is certain to cause discomfort between shifts. Other words that can be used to describe these aggravating maladies are "stinger," "pincher," or "burner."

Two-line pass

If a pass crosses both blue lines before it is received, then you have a two-line pass. In the case of a two-line pass, the official whistles the play dead and the puck is dropped in the offending team's zone.

Two-way player

A two-way player is recognized as being responsible at both ends of the ice and someone who can contribute with both defence and offence.

U V W

Unbalanced schedule

In an attempt to underline geographical rivalries and to lower teams' travel costs, the NHL now uses an unbalanced schedule. This schedule means that teams within the Eastern Conference will play each other anywhere from four to eight times, while playing Western Conference opponents once or perhaps not at all during the course of a season.

There has been a lot of controversy concerning the use of an unbalanced schedule. The biggest outcry has come from fans who are upset at not being able to see their favourite NHL stars. For example, fans of the Anaheim Ducks may wait years before having the opportunity to see exciting young superstars Sidney Crosby or Alexander Ovechkin in person under this type of schedule.

Unnecessary roughness

Hockey is a rough-and-tumble sport, but even in the sport of hockey you can carry the physicality a little too far. If a player gets a little too rambunctious with another player or if in the eyes of the officials he or she will not cease and desist, then the aggressor will receive a two-minute minor penalty.

Vintage jersey / third jersey

Most, if not all, teams in the NHL have a third or vintage jersey that they wear on special occasions. Usually the third jersey is a throwback jersey that honours a past team, or in the case of the Dallas Stars, a cultural symbol of its city.

Worst to first: The Vancouver Canucks may very well lay claim to having the worst and best vintage jerseys. While everyone can agree that the garish yellow "V" sweater of the early 1980s should never again see the light of day, the green-and-blue jersey of the 1970s with the subtle "rink and stick" emblem is a superb jersey and quickly becoming a fan favourite for Canuck fans.

Walk-on

A walk-on is the hockey player who goes undrafted and unsigned, and against all odds makes the roster despite having been snubbed. You have to love the athlete who refuses to believe all the naysayers and so-called experts and finds a place on the roster through hard work and determination.

WHL

The Western Hockey League is a Tier I Canadian major junior league and is a charter member of the Canadian Hockey League along with the OHL and the QMJHL. The WHL is made up of teams from the Canadian prairie provinces, British Columbia, and the western United States.

World Cup of Hockey

Although not as popular as soccer's World Cup, the World Cup of Hockey has nonetheless been a compelling event for hockey fans. There have been two World Cup tournaments. In 1996, the upstart USA team defeated Canada two games to one, while Canada would get its first World Cup of Hockey championship in 2004 with a victory over Finland.

Wrap around

Maple Leafs icon Mats Sundin may be the best ever at the wrap around. The term "wrap around" is used to describe a player going around one side of the net and coming out from behind the net on the other side and stuffing the puck past the goalie. The wrap around is especially tough on a keeper because once committed to stopping the shot on the strong side, the goalie is then forced to slide from one post to the other to prevent the wrap around on the other side.

Wrist shot

A type of shot that involves using arm muscles (especially those in the wrist and forearm) to propel the puck forward from the open faced, concave part of the hockey stick blade. The advantage of using a wrist shot as opposed to a slapshot is that it allows for an element of surprise and a quicker release since the windup is minimal.

XYZ

Zamboni

Developed in the 1940s by inventor Frank Zamboni, a Zamboni is a machine used to resurface the ice during intermissions and before shootouts.

Trivia Answers

Buds (page 8): In 1914 the Toronto Blueshirts won Toronto's first Stanley Cup championship.

Buzzer beater (page 9): Sergei Federov, in game six of the first round against goaltender Jon Casey and the Minnesota North Stars.

Captains (page 11): In today's game, keepers are not allowed to be captains. The last NHL goalie to be a captain was Montreal's Bill Durnan in 1948.

Cooperalls (page 16): For a brief while in the early 1980s both Philadelphia and Hartford made the Cooperalls part of their game-day attire.

Original Six (page 77): a2, b6, c1, d3, e4, f5.

Retired numbers (page 90): Number 99, of course! Wayne Gretzky retired as a player from pro hockey in April of 1999 and immediately the NHL decreed that no player would ever wear the number again in honour of the "Great One."

The Stopper (page 106): Claude Lemieux (1995), Scott Stevens (2000), and Anaheim's J. S. Giguere (2003).

The Triple Crown line (page 114): B) Darryl Sittler. The fact that the line of Dionne, Sittler, and McDonald was not Canada's best in the inaugural Canada Cup speaks to how talent-laden that team actually was. In the final game of the championship series against Czechoslovakia, Sittler accepted a nifty feed from Dionne in overtime and deposited it behind the Czech goalkeeper for the tournament winner.